WHEN A
GOOD MAN
FALLS

Distributed by:

Australia
Christian Press,
3 Harley Crescent,
Condell Park 2200,
Sydney,
Australia.

New Zealand
Gospel Publishing House Society Ltd.,
154 King Street,
PO Box 74,
Palmerston North,
New Zealand.

Singapore
Scripture Union Distributors,
413 Tagore Avenue,
Singapore 2678.

South Africa
Christian Art Wholesale,
20 Smuts Avenue,
Box 1599,
Vereeniging 1930,
South Africa.

WHEN A
GOOD MAN
FALLS

Erwin W. Lutzer

 **Scripture Press**

**AMERSHAM-ON-THE-HILL, BUCKS HP6 6JQ,
ENGLAND**

© 1988 by SP Publications, Inc.
First published in the USA 1988 by Victor Books a division
of Scripture Press Publications, Inc., Wheaton, Illinois, USA

First British edition 1989

ISBN 0 946515 73 5

Production and printing in Great Britain for
SCRIPTURE PRESS FOUNDATION (UK) LTD
Raans Road, Amersham-on-the-Hill, Bucks HP6 6JQ by
Nuprint Ltd, Harpenden, Herts AL5 4SE

Contents

Acknowlegment is made to my good friend, Les Stobbe, of San Bernardino, California, for his encouragement and valuable editorial assistance in making this book a reality.

AS YOU BEGIN

What happens when a good Christian falls into flagrant sin? Can he or she ever rise again, like the fabled phoenix, from the ashes of his or her spiritual defeat? If you took a poll in your church, what percentage would vote to give a repentant person another responsible position?

In addition to those questions, there are others we will consider. How does God respond to the faithful person who falls into a shameful sin? Should the curtain fall forever over his or her ministry? Has God ever used such a person again? Did God treat Old Testament saints differently because Jesus had not yet come? We are going to get the answers as we study the backsliding of twelve men from the Old Testament and the New Testament.

Think about the variety of backsliding presented in the Bible. There's the unshakable man of God, Noah, who built an ark for 120 years despite the jeers of his townspeople, yet he imbibed so freely of the fermented fruit of the vine that he lay naked in his tent. Years later the righteous man Lot (for *righteous* is what the Apostle Peter calls him) was saved from the unrighteous cities of Sodom and Gomorrah, only to commit incest while in a drunken stupor. And what happened to Moses when he committed manslaughter and then ran to hide in the desert?

Do you know that for forty years after his band of 300 defeated the Midianites, Gideon operated a worship center without Jehovah? That he took on numerous wives, with one son killing all his brothers? Having many foreign wives resulted in the backsliding of Solomon. It was the fear of what a good God would do that sent Jonah traveling in a direction opposite to the destination God had chosen for him. And we all know of the lustful life of Samson and how his life came to a resounding end.

One of the few good kings of Judah, Asa, served the Lord wholeheartedly for thirty-six years, only to enter into a fateful alliance with a Syrian king. That alliance cast a pall over Asa's last years as king. A New Testament disciple who made a bad alliance was Judas, who chose to join the side of the political/spiritual leaders of his day rather than suffer with Jesus.

Can anyone overlook Peter, who was not only a good fisherman but the kind of loyal disciple every leader needs? Yet Peter let a maidservant trip him into denying his Lord. And remember Demas, that New Testament follower of Paul, who one day in the pressure-cooker of Rome deserted the apostle.

That doesn't cover the backsliding of Abraham in Egypt, of David's double sin (adultery/murder), of Job's serious questioning of God's justice in his case, of John Mark's desertion of Paul and Barnabas on their first missionary journey.

Why did God include so many failures, so much backsliding, in the Bible? Because it is a record of God's redemptive purposes with those He created to serve Him. Repeatedly, many of the very people who chose the path of disobedience also again chose the path of obedience. And when they did that, God again blessed them. He forgives and forgets! He does restore the years the locusts have eaten.

This book is not merely a catalog of failures and defeats. Yes, we will examine those, including those who did not rebound from sin, but the goal here is to let you become aware of our gracious, forgiving God. Together we want to learn enough about our vulnerability to avoid the failures of others, enough about the forgiveness of God to be challenged to forgive others who have fallen, and enough about God's willingness to restore to give us courage and hope when we are repentant after being trapped by sin. You see, we want to learn more about God than about the failures of men.

1
MOSES
A Life Under Trial

Recently I received this letter:

> I am a man 31 years old and divorced, though I fought the divorce bitterly.
>
> I feel bad because I have no hope for the future; often I go home from church and cry. But there is no one to hold me when I cry. No one cares. What hurts most is that I've begged God for the grace to be single for His glory and to fix my eyes on Jesus, but nothing changes. I continue to fail.
>
> I am a basket case emotionally or on the verge of collapse. Something is very wrong. I'm so crippled and embittered that I can scarcely relate to others anymore. *I feel I have to sit out the rest of my life in the penalty box.*

The penalty box—have you been there?

Maybe it's a result of a bankruptcy you couldn't avoid, an ugly habit that brought health problems, or an immoral relationship that has blown over and you have tried to make things right. But you feel as if you are in the penalty box, much as in hockey when a player has to be out of the game for a rule infraction or flagrant misconduct. But do you have to stay there the rest of your life?

You've got a friend in Moses. He spent forty years in Pharaoh's court, another forty leading the Israelites out of Egypt, but sandwiched in between he spent another forty years in the penalty box for manslaughter.

Stephen tells us in Acts 7 that Moses was "educated in all the wisdom of the Egyptians and was powerful in speech and action" (v. 22). He had studied mathematics, astronomy, and chemistry, as well as hieroglyphics. The son of Pharaoh's daughter, he enjoyed the role of a celebrity who had every luxury Egypt could offer. F.B. Meyer speculates that when Moses rode forth into the streets, "it would be in a princely equipage amid the cries of, 'Bow the knee.' If he floated on the Nile, it would be in a golden barge, amid the strains of voluptuous music."

Josephus says that when the Ethiopians successfully invaded Egypt, Moses was put in charge of the royal troops. He surprised and defeated the enemy and returned with spoils of victory. As Meyer reminds, "The cream of Egypt was poured into his cup."

Although Moses was educated as an Egyptian, he remained an Israelite in his heart. Grief gripped him when he saw his people making bricks in the hot sun. He knew they had to work even harder after the Pharaoh told them that they had to gather their own straw. This child of luxury and fashion could have stayed in the palace, but he chose to take long walks keeping an eye on what was happening out in the fields. The mistreatment of his people made him deeply angry.

He knew he was called to be their deliverer. His mother had shared with him how God had preserved him in a basket along the Nile. What is more, he felt the compulsion of leadership: he could not rid himself of the impression that his destiny did not lie in the palace but in taking the risk of freeing his people. The special privileges he had were not to be wasted. He was a man of destiny.

One day he saw an Egyptian whipping an Israelite. This

was too much; the time for swift action had arrived. Moses looked around and when he saw no one watching, he killed the Egyptian and hid him in the sand (Ex. 2:12). The next day he went out to settle a quarrel among two Israelites, and he was surprised to hear the offender say, "Who made you ruler and judge over us? Are you thinking of killing me as you killed the Egyptian?" (v. 14)

Moses was stunned that someone had been watching when he killed the Egyptian. Though he had scanned the horizon carefully, apparently it wasn't carefully enough. Or else he hadn't covered the corpse with enough sand.

But something else bothered him even more deeply—his own people had rejected him. Stephen comments, "Moses thought that his own people would realize that God was using him to rescue them, but they did not" (Acts 7:25). He had *supposed* his people would understand! This was an unfortunate assumption. As hundreds of people who have failed in life have had to learn, it's often presumptious to suppose that God's people will understand!

Pharaoh felt betrayed by the one who grew up under his tutelage, so he wanted Moses dead. Likely, the Israelites would not have protected Moses even if they could have, so he had few options. In order to save his life, he fled to the desert.

To be hated by Pharaoh was understandable, but to be rejected by the people Moses risked his life to help created a wound that would take years to heal. Our disappointments seldom come from the world, but from the people of God from whom we expect understanding. As has often been said, Christians shoot their wounded!

When he got to Midian, Moses was exhausted, so he sat down beside a well. He had a box of medals; he was qualified to be the king of Egypt; but back in Egypt his reputation was forever ruined. Undoubtedly, Pharaoh let the people know what a traitor his adopted son had become.

Why all of this?

A Life Under Trial

Moses had to learn some lessons that success couldn't teach him. There is a transformation of character that can only take place in the desert. You can get an education in the palace, but wisdom comes in the desert.

What are we to learn when we are in the penalty box?

THE LESSON OF SERVANTHOOD

First of all, we must learn to serve. When the daughters of the priest of Midian came to the well, Moses protected them from rough shepherds and helped them draw water (Ex. 2:17). Though he had been trained for more prestigious responsibilities, he did whatever he could to help. The change was beginning to happen.

When Reuel, the father of the young women, asked who helped them, they knew only that they had met an Egyptian. The man who had instant recognition in Egypt was now doomed to live in obscurity and humiliation. He was invited to Reuel's home and married Zipporah, one of the man's daughters. And from then on he would be a shepherd.

Moses was miles from Egypt geographically and also socially. Shepherds were an abomination to the Egyptians. Now this prestigious child of fame and fortune would waste his life doing what the most unlettered slave could do as well as he. For forty years he did what he had formerly been taught to despise. When his wife bore him a son, they named him Gershom, which means "foreigner" (Ex. 2:22). Moses never did feel at home in the desert; he was like the proverbial square peg in a round hole. His aptitude lay in one direction, his responsibilities in another. His training appeared wasted.

As far as Moses was concerned, he expected to stay in the penalty box in Midian for the rest of his life. No one would ever be impressed with his credentials; he had nothing to do but to look on a mistake and contemplate how he had been treated. In the backside of the desert, nobody cared. There would be no promotions. At best he would graduate from one flock of sheep to another.

In Egypt, mothers had undoubtedly pointed to Moses and said to their sons, "There's Moses . . . be like him." But now no one admired his education or leadership. Yet God was teaching him to be faithful in obscurity. Francis Schaeffer said that there are no big people and no little people as far as God is concerned, only consecrated and unconsecrated people. That's why our vocation isn't as important to God as it is to us. There is fulfillment in obscurity, if we do it for Him. Yes, even when we are asked to do a job for which we are not suited, we can turn it into a delight if we believe we are doing it for God.

When Jacob went to work for Laban he agreed to serve seven years for Rachael. The text says, "But they seemed like only a few days to him because of his love for her" (Gen. 29:20). Even time goes more quickly when we serve with a right attitude!

Ruth Harms Calkin wrote:

You know, Lord, how I serve You
With great emotional fervor
In the limelight.
You know how eagerly I speak for You
At a women's club.
You know how I effervess when I promote
Fellowship groups.
You know my genuine enthusiasm at Bible study.
But how would I react
I wonder
If you pointed to a basin of water
And asked me to wash the calloused feet
Of a bent and wrinkled old woman
Day after day
Month after month
In a room where nobody saw
And nobody knew.

Servanthood is best learned in the desert. It happens when we are asked to do those things for which we are overqualified. Moses had to learn it's not *what* you do but *why* you do it that matters to God.

THE LESSON OF TRUST

Servanthood wasn't all that Moses had to learn. He had to remember that God is working even when His actions are imperceptible. "During that long period, the king of Egypt died. The Israelites groaned in their slavery and cried out, and their cry for help because of their slavery went up to God" (Ex. 2:23). In the course of many days, God began to work—14,600 days to be precise. It took forty years, but God began to answer the people's prayer.

There are three verbs that describe what God was doing. He *heard* the groaning of His people. He wasn't deaf after all. Though God didn't respond to His people's cries immediately, He was listening.

Next, God *remembered* His covenant. Though we may forget promises or even fail to deliver on those we remember, He is never careless with His commitments. For Him, time does not erase details; everything is fresh in His memory. That's why He will be able to evaluate us with such accuracy—He remembers precisely what happened way back in 1961 . . . 1956 . . . 1943!

One reason why we can forget the injustices that we experience is because God remembers them—and since He is the judge there is really no reason for us to have to remember them too! Moses was learning that even when life is slow and God is silent, He is fully aware of what's happening.

God also *saw* the needs of His people. He was feeling along with their hurts. Their ways were not hidden from Him, though deliverance was long in coming. For the moment, Moses had to learn to trust God even when God appeared to be indifferent regarding the needs of His people. Of course, it's easy to trust God when the bush is burning, the waters are parting, and the mountains are shaking—it's those silent years that are discouraging.

Yes, it's easy to talk about faith when you're healthy and the boss has just promoted you. When you are happy with your work and your children are following the Lord, trust comes easily. But when you've been misunderstood, misrepresented, and when you're in a job that is not suited to your abilities or training, when you've got medical bills and an impossible marriage partner, that's when trust means most to God. It's in the desert and not in the palace that God finds out the depths of our yieldedness. It's when He is silent, not when He speaks, that our faith is precious in His sight.

Moses was learning—and so must we.

THE LESSON OF OBEDIENCE

God came to Moses in the burning bush and told him that it was time to get out of the penalty box and back into the game. For starters, Moses replied, "Who am I, that I should go to Pharaoh and bring the Israelites out of Egypt?" (Ex. 3:11)

Moses was a different man. Forty years before, he had thought he could pull off the Exodus in his own strength, but now he had learned his lesson We might expect him to have said to God, "Where have *You* been? I've been just waiting to return to Egypt." But he asked the question that anyone who has been broken by God would ask: "Who am I, that I should go to Pharaoh and bring the Israelites out of Egypt?" He had been crushed and hurt. This is the point to which God wants to bring each of us; it's the question of a man who has seen himself for what he is. A.W. Tozer has said that the best leaders are not those who want the job but those who are conscripted by God for leadership. At last, Moses qualified.

For God, of course, Moses' limitations were not an obstacle. He answered, "Certainly I will be with you. . . . " But Moses was still hurting. Though he was in the desert for forty years, he still could not forget that his people had re jected him. Perhaps he even preferred that they rot in Egypt! When you're in the penalty box, it's easy to become bitter.

So Moses comes up with a second excuse, "What if they do not believe me or listen to me and say, 'The Lord did not appear to you'?" (Ex. 4:1) Moses was wondering whether he would be rejected again. How did God overcome Moses' hurt? He asked, "What is in your hand?" Moses replied, "A staff." Then God enabled Moses to do special miracles with it. When he threw it on the ground, it became a serpent, but when he stretched out his hand and caught its tail, it was transformed back into a staff. From then on, Moses carried this staff with him and it was used by God in defeating the Egyptians. That slender piece of wood, about five feet long, would be a constant reminder to Moses that God would be with him all the way. The rod of Moses became the rod of God.

And where did Moses get this rod? While serving in the penalty box, of course. Later he would stretch out his rod over the sea and the waters would part. Again, he would be reminded of his days in the desert.

Eventually, God overcame Moses' objections. The reluctant Moses was pressed back into service. He was now qualified to do what he had attempted earlier in his own strength.

Today, God asks you and me, "What is in *your* hand? What have you learned while on the sidelines?" Patience faith, the ability to love the unlovable? Have you learned to be content in obscurity, to trust God in adversity? Has shame brought bitterness or brokenness? David, who spent his share of time recouping from failure, said, "The sacrifices of God are a broken spirit; a broken and contrite heart, O God, you will not despise" (Ps. 51:17).

A pastor fell into the sin of immorality. When his sin

became known, his reputation was ruined, his career seemingly over. He found a job in a warehouse, an occupation for which he was, to put it mildly, overqualified. Only a few Christian friends stood by him through the experience. No one dared recommend him to another church, though he had repented. Gifted, educated, qualified for ministry, he was now a nobody, rejected, obscure. He could have become bitter, but he began to serve God where he was. He began attending a church—first as a visitor, then as a member, and within time he became a Sunday School teacher. He was faithful in what he did, spending much time being quiet before God.

A year went by, then another. God began to give him greater ability, more opportunities. "God loves to hurt His people," he would say. "It's the branch that bears fruit that feels the pruning knife." Today this man is out of the penalty box and has an effective ministry.

Not every story, of course, has such a happy ending. But if we learn our lessons in the desert, we'll find it's not really a penalty box at all—it's really God's training ground for a deeper, less self-centered ministry. There is a new touch of God that comes in the desert.

Moses had to learn that God delights in making servants, not Pharaohs. And He can do His best work in obscurity, not in the limelight.

Don't let Satan talk you into wasting your failures. God is with you in the penalty box to teach you to serve, trust, and obey.

To be sidelined is not a waste of time if you get private tutoring from the Coach.

2

JONAH

Struggling Against God

Have you ever deliberately disobeyed God? Perhaps on an impulse you went out and did something you knew was sinful. Maybe you refused to forgive someone or you rebelled against your parents' wishes in order to do your thing. Then again, you may have rejected God's prompting to be a missionary to another culture.

How would you react if your disobedience was written up in a local newspaper? Now imagine that it also was recorded in stone so that archeologists 2,000 years from now could say, "Look at this story. Here's a person who willfully disobeyed God. He was so bigoted he wouldn't befriend a Hispanic alien."

That's what happened to the most prominent prophet of God living in Israel during the reign of Jeroboam II. Not only was the story of Jonah's prejudice recorded as part of the history of his day, but it was given by God as a lesson for all time in His Word, the Bible.

Jonah must have been a particularly effective prophet for God to entrust him with warning the residents of Nineveh, the capital of Assyria. They had a reputation as a particularly cruel race, who committed the most horrible atrocities on their enemies. A prophet would have to have

Struggling Against God

steel in his soul to warn them about God's judgment! So when God said to Jonah, "Go to the great city of Nineveh and preach against it, because its wickedness has come up before Me" (Jonah 1:2), we should not be surprised at Jonah's response.

His problem? He was upset with God's will for him. In effect, he was saying, "I find the will of God distasteful. I want those Assyrians punished before they decide to turn on God and eventually fight against us. Enemies they are, and you don't warn enemies of coming judgment."

We will never know in this life if Jonah actually thought he could escape God's long arm by heading in the opposite direction from Nineveh. We do know that he went to the port city of Joppa and bought a ticket for Tarshish. In doing so, he discovered three significant lessons that every good man who falls must learn when he deliberately gets off course.

What were those lessons that completed Jonah's education?

WHEN YOU RUN, GOD PURSUES YOU

Jonah fled to Tarshish . . . "from the Lord" (1:3) The Hebrew literally means that Jonah was running away from "the face of the Lord." He wanted to get out of the range of God's eye. As he ran, he went *down* to Joppa, *down* to Tarshish and *down* into the ship, and eventually *down* into the belly of the fish (1:3-17). Running away from God means that you inevitably go *down*, never up.

But Jonah discovered that you cannot travel incognito when trying to run away from God. There was an invisible Presence right on his heels. Regardless of how far he ran, the Lord was with him.

God pursued Jonah in two ways. First, God got Jonah's attention through circumstances. "Then the Lord sent a great wind on the sea, and such a violent storm arose that the ship threatened to break up" (1:4). The storm broke after Jonah had disappeared into the hold of the ship for a nap, and the winds frightened the wits out of the crew.

Clearly, the average person in Jonah's day would not have seen the connection between the storm and the prophet's flight. Nor does the average person today see God using circumstances to trip up the fleeing young person from a godly family but who wants "freedom." Certainly not all tragedies are the result of sin, but some are.

As the winds howled and waves pounded the ship, the sailors began by calling on their gods to stop the storm. At this point Jonah was still asleep at the bottom of the ship—an indication that the person who is out of fellowship with God may sleep as well as ever. We can shut feelings of guilt and alienation out of our consciousness for a long period of time—and sleep helps.

In the case of Jonah, his greatest problem was not with the pagans but with himself, the prophet of God! Sometimes when we look at the storm into which God is taking our country, we blame the humanists and Communists. Could it be, however, that the storms that God sends are because of backslidden Christians asleep, oblivious to the high wind?

Let's give the pagans on Jonah's ship credit for trying to keep the ship afloat. Sometimes even those who do not know the Lord are doing their best to restore a sense of balance to our morally disjointed nation. In Jonah's case you can see the "Christian" asleep while God is about to speak through unconverted sailors.

After the lot falls on Jonah, he says, "Throw me overboard." He knew it was his fault and he was willing to face up to it. Have you ever thought of how stubborn Jonah was? When he was thrown overboard, he expected to drown in the Mediterranean Sea. To him, death was more attractive than obedience to the will of God.

I've met Christians like that. I think of a wife to whom suicide is more attractive than living with her husband.

Struggling Against God

Many people would prefer to join the 25,000 Americans a year who take their own life, than to face the reality of obedience to God.

Perhaps you are running from God either geographically or morally. You know what is right but refuse to do it—or you know what is wrong and do it anyway. You may not have realized it until now, but God is pursuing you. Nothing you can do can get you out from under His constant gaze. Regardless of how far and how long you run, God goes with you.

Jonah learned a second lesson.

WHEN YOU REPENT, GOD HEARS YOU

Suddenly Jonah found that he had exchanged a ship's belly for a fish's belly. By now he was ready to call on God. His environment was a rather confined creative learning center. But God now had the prophet's complete attention.

There in the belly of the fish Jonah rediscovered prayer. He said to himself, "This business of running from God is not working out very well. I think I should get back into fellowship." Read his confession in Jonah 2:1-9, where he recognizes that God was with him even in the midst of his predicament.

He says in verse 4, "I have been banished from your sight; yet I will look again toward Your holy temple" (2:4). In the Old Testament sense, Jonah was a believer. He did not have to get saved again, but he did have to bounce back into fellowship.

Jonah spoke of going back to the temple, back to the place where he started drifting away from God. Whenever we return, we have to return to the point where we lost our way. In speaking to one backslider who asked me, "Where do I begin?" I answered, "What sin was more important to you than the will of God? Though you have been running from God for three years, what got you off course?" Often pondering that question helps us understand why we lost our way and how we can begin again.

God accepted Jonah's repentance and renewed his assignment. "Then the Word of the Lord came to Jonah a second time: 'Go to the great city of Nineveh and proclaim to it the message I give you' " (Jonah 3:1-2).

Recently, a man in his fifties came to me and said, "Pastor, I feel as if I've ruined my life. I've had a bad marriage; my children are not walking with the Lord. Is it ever too late to begin?" I was delighted to tell him that it is never too late to do what is right!

Remember the parable Jesus told in which the man who was hired at 5:30 P.M. was paid as much as those who showed up at 9 in the morning? Of course the earlybirds grumbled. But the owner of the vineyard reminded them that they had agreed to work for a denarius. But they still grumbled. The landowner asked one of the grumblers, "Don't I have the right to do what I want with my own money? Or are you envious because I am generous?' " (Matt. 20:15)

Yes, God is generous and He can do as He wishes with His own. I've seen God take people who repented after many wasted years and use them mightily in His kingdom. God does some truly marvelous things in the lives of the 5:30 P.M. arrivals. Never underestimate what God can do with a restored backslider!

Finally, Jonah took his sermon notes and preached in Nineveh. I find this part of the story harder to believe than the part about Jonah being swallowed by a fish. Consider why we might not expect him to get any positive results. For one thing, the time limit was restricted. Forty days? Who ever heard of a revival in forty days where there had not been an advance man and prayer cells in all the blocks of the city? Those things take time, especially in a pagan environment.

Then consider the preacher. He did not want the people to repent, so his sermons hardly had the ring of sincerity.

Finally, consider the message. There was no grace, just

a prediction of terror. What kind of results would that kind of preaching get today?

Once again we see the grace of God. I remember speaking to a man who thought he could never repent. Later I discovered he was guilty of murder. Can he be restored to God? Yes, and I'm glad to say that he was.

The second lesson that Jonah learned is that God listens to the backslider who repents.

WHEN YOU COMPLAIN, GOD TEACHES YOU

The closing chapter of Jonah contains a stunning surprise. Even though the prophet had an earth-shaking revival, he was greatly displeased. Six hundred thousand people repented. Even the animals were clothed in sackcloth. Yet, Jonah was angry.

"He prayed to the Lord, 'Lord, is this not what I said when I was still at home? That is why I was so quick to flee to Tarshish. I knew that You are a gracious and compassionate God, slow to anger and abounding in love, a God who relents from sending calamity' " (Jonah 4:2).

Instead of doing follow-up work, he's thinking, "Lord, I hope they never get discipled so that their repentance won't last and You'll have to judge them."

Jonah then sank into such depression that he longed to die. "Now, O Lord, take away my life, for it is better for me to die than to live" (4:3). Like a student who's flunked his final exams, he just wanted to die in his sleep and get it over with. Once again, suicide was more attractive than facing reality.

Now God gave Jonah an object lesson; He appointed a plant to cover Jonah's head. The huge leaves would provide more cooling than the shelter Jonah had erected. By evaporation the big leaves gave off moisture. Understandably, Jonah was happy about the plant.

God is our comfort today as well. He put that roof over your head and provided the clothes you wear. In fact, Paul says that the goodness of God leads us to repentance. He appoints the comforts of life. But in order for us to realize what God is doing for us, He sometimes takes those comforts away. In the case of Jonah, He sent a worm that sawed the plant down during the night.

God was saying to Jonah, "I am the God of your comforts but also the God of your disappointments. I gave you the plant, but I also took it away. Both the plant and the worm are My instruments."

And God wasn't finished yet. Next He "provided a scorching east wind, and the sun blazed on Jonah's head so that he grew faint. He wanted to die and said, 'It would be better for me to die than live' " (4:8).

God gave Jonah a taste of a blast furnace, knowing that if anything will bring out the worst in us it is bad weather! The hot scorching east wind dried not only the sweat on Jonah's face but also his shriveling heart.

Notice that three times the same descriptive verb is used to highlight God's hand in the experiences of life. God *provided* the plant; He *provided* a worm; He *provided* a scorching east wind. God takes full responsibility for the comforts, disappointments, and tragedies of life. All are equally appointed. Blessed is the person who can see all experiences as originating from His loving hand!

And now God gives His final word to the prophet. "But the Lord said, 'You have been concerned about this vine, though you did not tend it or make it grow. It sprang up overnight and died overnight. But Nineveh has more than a hundred and twenty thousand people who cannot tell their right hand from their left, and many cattle as well. Should I not be concerned about that great city?" (4:10-11) God was saying, "I have a heart of compassion. I wanted the people in this city to repent and here you are, all bent out of shape because you disagreed with Me and don't like the weather in Nineveh. You'd rather have Me put a plant over your head to give you shade than to see these people repent and be saved!"

Struggling Against God

That is the heart of the backslider, the Christian who has fallen into sin and is in rebellion against God. It's then that we get selfish, bigoted, parochial, uncaring—in a word, self-centered.

We can have the same feelings about our city too. We can sit in the shade of a suburban home until a tornado comes like the worm in Jonah's day. And we can get angry at God about the terrible weather because He has made life uncomfortable for us.

But while the Book of Jonah teaches us much about the human heart, it really is a commentary on the grace of God. Just think of what lengths God will go to bring a backslidden prophet into fellowship! And, of course, He had no trouble with the fish . . . with the wind . . . with the storm . . . with the plant . . . with the worm. It's the man that digs in his heels and says, "I won't."

I have seen God drag Christians from one brierpatch to another, kicking and screaming. He is trying to get their attention, to let them know that He cares. All He wants is to hear them say, "Lord, I am out of step. I'll march to Your drumbeat." Instead, they get bent out of shape over some of the most trivial issues of life. They've lost their vision, compassion, and burden for others.

Where is God for the backslidden Christian, the good man who has fallen? He is waiting in love and mercy . . . waiting for him to leave his rebellion and pettiness and bow humbly before God in faith and obedience.

Perhaps you feel you've been in the belly of a fish for a long time, but God is waiting to put you back on His pleasant shore if you pray the prayer of repentance that Jonah voiced to God. And remember to go back to the "temple" where you once met God.

He has an assignment for you.

3
<u>LOT</u>

The Cost of Selfish Ambitions

Initially, sin seems like a bargain. Its allurement is unmistakable. Yet throughout history the record is clear—there are no bargains where sin is concerned. And Lot, a highly honored city dweller of early biblical history, presents a truly striking example of its high cost.

The stage is set in Genesis, chapter 13. The scene opens with wealthy Abraham taking Lot, a nephew he had apparently adopted as his son, into Canaan from Egypt via the Negev. At Bethel and Ai, Abraham proclaimed his allegiance to Jehovah by building an altar and calling upon the Lord in public worship.

God's blessing upon Abraham and his nephew produced seeds of conflict. The grazing lands were inadequate for both of their animals and a confrontation between their herdsmen erupted. As the head of the family, Abraham suggested a peace plan.

"Look," he said, "there's plenty of land, so why don't we put a little distance between us." To quote the biblical writer, "Let's not have any quarreling between you and me, or between your herdsmen and mine, for we are brothers. Is not the whole land before you? Let's part company. If you go to the left, I'll go to the right; if you go

The Cost of Selfish Ambitions

to the right, I'll go to the left" (Gen. 13:8-9).

When Lot's eyes swept over the valley of the Jordan, he knew what part of Canaan would best feed his flocks—and his ambition. No doubt about it, the area was well-watered; it looked like the garden of the Lord, as fruitful as the most productive area of Egypt from which he and Abraham had recently come. So he chose it, leaving the less productive area to his uncle. The hidden costs of that selfish choice were to be revealed only later.

For the moment, Lot seems to have forgotten that God had promised Abraham the whole territory (12:7). Technically, of course, Lot had every right to choose as he did. After all, Abraham made a bona fide offer. Yet as we all know, not all that is legal is actually right. Lot's choice was based on his vision of cattle grazing in lush pasturelands, rather than his understanding of God's plan. His only goal was success, and his covetousness cost him far more than he bargained for.

LOT—THE OPPORTUNIST

But before we find out what the hidden costs were, let's sit down with Lot for an interview. We're at the gate of Sodom, where Lot lives, watching a parade of donkeys and camels laden with precious goods. Pedestrians dart here and there with excitement and determination. We set up a microphone and ask, "Lot, you were one of the wealthiest cattle and sheep ranchers in all of Canaan. Why did you give up that pastoral life?"

"Opportunity, my friend, opportunity."

"Exactly what kind of opportunity?"

"The opportunity to improve the return on my investment," Lot responds. "After all, you can do precious little business talking to sheep. Even if you increase their number, the life of a shepherd is rather confined. I enjoy being with people, and so do my wife and family."

"I understand, but what else attracted you to Sodom?"

"In the city I have found opportunity to grow in respect, to gain a reputation as a successful businessman. The Lord has given me many gifts, and this was one way to use them. What is more, my wife enjoys the social occasions that we have here."

"As I look around me, sir, it seems to me that your present position as a judge in the gate represents another kind of opportunity."

"True, true," responds Lot. "This is very affirming. Here I can apply all of the accumulated wisdom of my fathers. Some people call me an opportunist. But you know, you really do need to look after yourself. And I am determined to write more than one page of the history of this city. For many generations the record will show that Lot helped make this city great."

For now we are impressed. But before we draw any conclusions on Lot's decision, let's find out how much it cost him. Genesis chapter 19 reveals three payments that Lot was eventually to make for this lush pastureland. They were the hidden costs of his self-interest.

IT COST HIS TESTIMONY

Though he had been reared on the plains, young Lot was attracted to urban life. Recall that after leaving Abraham, he pitched his tent in the valley and rather quickly moved closer to Sodom. Genesis 19:1 begins a shocking account: "Now the two angels came to Sodom in the evening as Lot was sitting in the gate of Sodom" (NASB). As already mentioned, he had achieved not only his material goals but also his social and political ambitions. He had arrived! Yet at this moment he did not know the cost.

The first payment Lot made for his selfish decision was the loss of his testimony in Sodom. The fact that he had worked his way up to become one of Sodom's leading citizens indicates that he was no longer a threat to their immoral way of life.

The Cost of Selfish Ambitions

"Lot," they must have said, "we like you. You were smart to give up that nomadic existence because you have the gifts of leadership that we need here. And because you are a shrewd businessman, we're willing to give you a place of honor at the city gate."

The prophetic voice calling people to repentance is strangely muted when you get to sit with the big men in town.

Evidently, Lot not only didn't witness to his friends in Sodom, but even his own family had not been taught the way of the Lord. When a mob came seeking the two angels who had come to him for a visit, he was willing to let his two virgin daughters be sexually abused by them. He actually addressed his friends as "brother" when they tried to beat down his door to get to the angels (19:7).

Take note: You do not get honored in Sodom unless you have decided to be quiet about your faith in Jehovah. You simply blend into the background of the big city and pay for your success by losing your testimony.

Many years later Jesus was to say, "If anyone is ashamed of Me and My words in this adulterous and sinful generation, the Son of Man will be ashamed of Him when He comes in His Father's glory with the holy angels" (Mark 8:38). The Apostle John wrote, "And now, dear children, continue in Him, so that when He appears we may be confident and unashamed before Him at His coming" (1 John 2:28).

The message is unmistakable. If we are so well thought of by the world that we compromise our testimony, we have paid too much for our success. Fading worldly glory does not begin to compare to the approval of Jesus Christ at His coming. But Lot had yet more to pay.

IT COST HIS FAMILY

Recently, a politician told his wife that she would have to accept the fact that she and the children would come second or third in his list of priorities. Lot made a similar payment to climb the social ladder in Sodom. He did it at the expense of his family. We've already noted that he was willing to sacrifice his two daughters by giving them to the mob and was saved only by the intervention of the angels. Apparently, Lot had other daughters who did not make it out of Sodom. We read, "So Lot went out and spoke to his sons-in-law, who were pledged to marry his daughters. He said, 'Hurry and get out of this place, because the Lord is about to destroy the city!' But his sons-in-law thought he was joking" (Gen. 19:14). Here's a man who had lost such credibility with his sons-in-law that they treated his message as a joke. The most serious moment of his life was ridiculed by his children, who in effect said, "Dad, you can't be for real!"

Yes, he did take two daughters with him when he fled the city. But though they were spared physically, Lot had lost them spiritually—they had absorbed the moral values of Sodom.

Lot lost his wife too. The angels had told him, "Hurry! Take your wife and your two daughters who are here, or you will be swept away when the city is punished. . . . Don't look back, and don't stop anywhere in the plain" (19:15, 17). But Lot's wife looked back and became a pillar of salt. For as they were leaving, God ignited Sodom and Gomorrah and all of the sulfur in that region exploded and descended upon the cities. They were totally consumed. And because she looked back, Lot's wife participated in that judgment.

Lot and his wife had invested heavily in Sodom. They likely had a beautiful home and belonged to the best social clubs. To leave all of that behind proved more than she could handle. Despite the explicit command, she disobeyed. Lot lost again.

How much did Lot pay for that move into Sodom? No money—but it cost him his witness, his children, and his family. That's a lot to pay for making it to the top. Yet

The Cost of Selfish Ambitions

because we pay for sin on the installment plan, Lot still had more to pay.

IT COST HIM HIS CHARACTER

The bad news continues. The biblical historian isn't even stopping to catch his breath. Lot ended up in a cave inebriated. His daughters served him so much wine he lost all his moral inhibitions and committed incest with them. The results of that sin were profound: "The older daughter had a son, and she named him Moab; he is the father of the Moabites of today. The younger daughter also had a son, and she named him Ben-Ammi; he is the father of the Ammonites of today" (Gen. 19:37-38).

Not many years later the Moabite women were seducing the Israelites and bringing God's judgment on Israel as they traveled into Canaan (Num. 25:1-3) and the Ammonites introduced the worship of Moloch to Israel, demanding the sacrifice of children on the altar.

If we could interview Lot now, what a different perspective he would have. The day he made the choice for the best pastureland he had no idea where he would end up. The choice seemed so innocent, so right, but it was so close to Sodom. Only later was it clear that the cost was disproportionate to the benefits.

And what was the root cause of Lot's selfish decision? What made him such a good citizen of Sodom? He felt at home there because he was cut from the same piece of cloth—he was covetous. Often we stress the immorality of Sodom, but God gives a different reason why the city was judged, "As surely as I live, declares the Sovereign Lord, your sister Sodom and her daughters never did what you and your daughters have done. Now this was the sin of your sister Sodom: She and her daughters were arrogant, overfed, and unconcerned; they did not help the poor and needy. They were haughty and did detestible things before Me" (Ezek. 16:48-50).

Of course we shouldn't overlook the moral abominations in Sodom and Gomorrah. But it was the arrogant affluence of the people that caused eventual judgment. It was because of the love of ease and pleasure that God set the cities ablaze.

God calls covetousness idolatry. It's undoubtedly the chief sin of America, whose economic policies resulted in a 28 percent jump in the number of poor between 1979 and 1982. The middle class is shrinking while the number of poor increase. And the selfishness of the rich, displayed in their unwillingness to share with the poor, is an abomination to God.

LEARNING FROM LOT'S EXPERIENCES

What do we learn from Lot's experience? First, God sets the price for sin. And this price is nonnegotiable.

For Lot, the pleasure of moving into Sodom was more important than any sense of guilt he may have felt over leaving his uncle with poorer pasturelands. Yet no matter how pleasant the diversion, God always sets the price for selfishness—and it is always higher than the offsetting value of self-gratification. Alcoholics, thieves, and adulterers—if pressed to be honest— would all agree. And even if they don't reach this conclusion on earth, they most assuredly will in eternity.

Second, there is a lesson of hope. God is able to deliver His people as He did Lot. Isn't that a contradiction? Yes, we have been stressing the price of sin in Lot's life, but that doesn't mean he had lost his standing before God. As previously pointed out, Peter refers to Lot as a righteous man, who was rescued by God. Lot's life was . . . "distressed by the filthy lives of lawless men (for that righteous man, living among them day after day, was tormented in his righteous soul by the lawless deeds he saw and heard)" (2 Peter 2:7-8).

Despite his compromises, Lot still had an active con-

The Cost of Selfish Ambitions

science. He remembered the devotion of his uncle Abraham. Yet Lot was not willing to make a clean break.

The writer of Scripture uses God's dramatic intervention into Lot's life and adds, "Then the Lord knows how to rescue the godly from temptation, and to keep the unrighteous under punishment for the day of judgment" (2 Peter 2:9, NASB). God may have to do the same for us today, possibly through the hand of a friend or a loved one. He graciously walks us out of our environment of sin so that we can escape the final judgment to come.

Many Christians will be saved but singed. The Apostle Paul says that we shall all stand before the Judgment Seat of Christ, and our works shall be tried with fire. Some will find their works all burned, but they themselves shall be saved as by fire (1 Cor. 3:15). The imagery is that of a burning house. As it collapses the person escapes through the door clad only in a nightgown. Everything else goes up in smoke.

Lot represents those who will be saved but will have nothing to show for their deeds. The cost of sin includes the loss of eternal rewards.

There is a final lesson. We are to rescue those who have sold out to Sodom. Jude wrote that we should "snatch others from the fire and save them" (v. 23). We are to hate the very garment spotted by sinful flesh, but we should rescue those who have become comfortable from the world.

Let's ask ourselves what we are doing to help alcoholics, homosexuals, and those who have fallen morally. It's not enough to preach against these vices; we must lend a helping hand. Some believers today are vexed with their own sinfulness but don't know the way out.

Today God sends His "angels"—fellow believers—to help His people get out of Sodom. And once they leave, they should never look behind.

Maybe you feel trapped by some sin just as Lot did. Your family and friends have become such a part of the world that you cannot bear the thought of breaking free. Just imagine the resistance Lot would have had if he had told his wife and family that he was leaving Sodom to go back to nomadic life. He would have soon found that *it's one thing to take a family out of Sodom and quite another to take Sodom out of a family!* Yet regardless of the protests, Lot would have been wise to do so. And if he had taken that decisive step, God would have helped him along the way.

Perhaps you are looking for an angel to rescue you from your environment or sinful habits. God may use a fellow Christian, your pastor, or a close friend. Yet you must reach out your hand so that you can be pulled free of the impending judgment. It's that hand of faith that God will honor.

Sodom represents any part of the world that has made a nest in your heart. If that is the case, God is waiting for you to repent so that He can cancel those payments that will eventually have to be made.

4

NOAH

The Snare of Alcoholism

Everyone of us remembers a kind uncle or grandfather who took a special interest in us when we were children. He was our ideal of a good man, a person who could be trusted and loved. Then perhaps one day in our teens we discovered that he ran around with evil women or did not tell the truth. Suddenly our idol was smashed. We wished we had never heard about his faults.

That's how I feel about Noah. He's everything I always wanted to be! He obeyed God with unquestioned loyalty and found grace in the eyes of the Lord. He had enough faith to fill the ark with a collection of living creatures that would make a modern zookeeper ecstatic. His vibrant faith infected his family, and they all joined him in the ark.

Why did God not let the story end with the ark sitting on dry land, and Noah offering a sacrifice to God? Why did He not leave us with a picture of Noah and his family that would be satisfying? We want our heroes to stay heroic. Yet that is not God's approach to biography; He tells it like it is!

That's one reason why we believe the Bible is the Word of God. If man had written the Scriptures, he would have done as Mary Ellen White did. Doug Hakleman reports,

The Snare of Alcoholism

"In her history of the Reformers, she presented me with these flawless men. But I knew enough by then about them to know that Martin Luther . . . wasn't perfect, like he was presented. Then I looked at the Old Testament biographies and saw men and women with all their warts and flaws. No covering up what they were" (*San Bernadino Sun,* April 7, 1984, p. D-7). As a result Hackleman decided that the Bible could be trusted as a valid message from God.

When you meet Noah in Genesis 6, you'd never guess that he'd be drunk in Genesis 9. When we are introduced to him, we find that he is the only person whom God could trust to fulfill His purposes. "Noah was a righteous man, blameless among the people of his time, and he walked with God" (Gen. 6:9).

Noah's first and last thoughts were always about God. Immediately after exiting from the ark, he "built an altar to the Lord, and taking some of the clean animals and clean birds, he sacrificed burnt offerings on it" (Gen. 8:20).

What was God's reaction? "The Lord smelled the pleasing aroma and said in His heart, 'Never again will I curse the ground because of man, even though every inclination of his heart is evil from childhood. And never again will I destroy all living creatures as I have done' " (Gen. 8:21).

Noah was not only righteous in the sight of God, he also had a credible reputation among the people of his day. They could not pin a single wrong action on him. He was blameless. No niece or nephew was ever disappointed in his conduct. Though he was thrust onto the front pages of his day's newspaper as a preacher of righteousness, he did not flinch when the criticism came. No doubt he was called a fool and worse, but he went on believing and working. God had said to Noah, "I am going to put an end to all people, for the earth is filled with violence. . . . I am surely going to destroy both them and the earth" (Gen. 6:13). Day by day he attached boards to the superstructure that would become the ark, his work reinforcing his message.

For 120 years he shared God's warning with others.

Yet one day Noah fell into sin. His one act began a progression of other sins in the life of his family. What a reminder that it's possible for seasoned saints to stumble in the sunset years of their life.

NOAH'S SIN

With all the commendations that Noah received from God one would think he would be above the battle of the passions. But one day the unmentionable happened (at least in most churches the sin of drunkenness is not spoken about except in hushed tones). This man of God who had demonstrated unfailing faith in God planted a vineyard, pressed his own grapes, let the juice turn into wine, and drank enough to become drunk. He was lying indecently exposed when his son walked in unannounced.

What a reminder that even godly people can be tripped just before the finish line. Young Christians particularly are often devastated when they discover the sins of their spiritual heroes. They say, "All these people in church have believed God for ten, fifteen, or even twenty-five years. They probably never get angry or become discouraged. They're praising the Lord all the time—they must be next to the angels." Then suddenly it happens—they find out that one of these dear saints has committed adultery, become drunk, or been dishonest in business.

Despite 120 years of following God, Noah was not ready to be fitted for angel wings. As he sat drinking wine alone in his dwelling, he exhibits the typical pattern of the secret drinker, the person who is involved in church but whose private world is unknown to the congregation.

Recently a wife confessed that she'd been covering for her alcoholic husband for years. She would phone the office and report that he was ill. Other lies were invented to explain her husband's negligence to the family and the people of the church. Yes, this may be common, but this woman's husband was a respected elder in a good evangelical church.

What a mistake to think that those who drink to excess are only on Skid Row. Only 2 percent of all alcoholics end up there—the rest are in offices, factories, churches, and homes. Though they are loathe to admit it, such alcoholics face life by having one drink after another. Mel Trotter, who became one of the great Skid Row mission leaders, tells of going to his little girl's coffin and removing her shoes to sell them for one more drink.

If all the closet alcoholics suddenly identified themselves in church some Sunday morning, we'd all be stunned. Many Christians know what it's like to have a consuming desire for another drink. It's a problem we can no longer self-righteously ignore.

The Rev. Bill Seath, for many years head of the Chicago Industrial League, is quoted as saying, "The number one reason for the increase in alcoholism is the rapid degeneration of the home environment over the past several generations. Parents are not teaching their children to fear alcohol, but are trying to teach them to drink like ladies and gentlemen, with moderation. With attitudes like this in the home, is it any wonder more and more children are becoming alcoholics before they even receive their high school diplomas?" (*How to Live with an Alcoholic and Win*, by Jim and Cyndy Hunt, p. 19)

If it happened to Noah, it can happen to anyone. Though some Christians argue that it's possible to drink in moderation, let's remember that one out of every four people who start to drink eventually become alcoholics. And we can't predict who that one in four will be.

Let's not excuse Noah by believing, as some commentators suggest, that he learned by accident that wine produces drunkenness. In Matthew 24:38 we read that one of the characteristics of Noah's day was that they were eating and drinking and giving in marriage. Surely, Noah was not so busy building an ark that he did not learn about the intoxicating nature of wine from his contemporaries! God let this story be in the Bible as a warning to all of us about the danger of drunkenness.

Noah's experience illustrates that drunkenness and immodesty usually go hand in hand. This is the first instance of drunkenness in the Bible and there you have it—Noah is lying naked in his tent. Alcoholism always lowers a person's moral defenses. After a few drinks, inhibitions are gone and reasonable people feel free to do what would be normally too embarrassing. Recently, I overheard a man discuss his immoral exploits, saying, "We had some drinks and then we. . . . " Alcohol enables people to act like animals without feeling bad about it. Far from drowning their problems, alcoholics find that drink only irrigates them!

Noah's sin reminds us that anyone can stumble into sin. But it also illustrates that when we fall, we usually take someone else with us. Remember those three-legged races at picnics? When you fall down, your partner does too—there's no such thing as sinning alone.

THE SIN OF NOAH'S SON

Up to this point in the story, we would think that Ham would be a fine son, someone Noah could really be proud of. He, along with his other two brothers, helped his dad build the ark, get the animals into it, and care for them. Undoubtedly, he also endured the ridicule of the people of that day. But there's no hint of any resistance or rebellion.

On the day Noah got drunk and passed out, we find an interesting sidelight about Ham, the oldest son. The Bible reports that "Noah lay uncovered inside his tent. Ham, the father of Canaan, saw his father's nakedness and told his two brothers outside" (Gen. 9:21-22). As a result a curse came upon Canaan the son of Ham.

What really was wrong with walking into the tent unexpectedly? Obviously, it wasn't the fact that Ham stumbled upon his father in an unclothed state. Rather,

The Snare of Alcoholism

Ham delighted in the shame of his father. One of the commentators translates the passage, "He told his brethren with delight."

Apparently, a root of rebellion had sprouted in Ham's heart which lay undetected up to this time. Even the godly life of Noah had not uprooted it; even the miracle of the Flood with its impending message of judgment did not teach Ham the need for respect and decency. To delight in someone else's wickedness is to be a willing participant in that sin.

Even fine families produce rebellious children. Yes, a godly environment helps, but the heart of man is deceitful above all things and desperately wicked. Without genuine repentance and commitment to the lordship of Christ, a root of sin can suddenly grow when the conditions are favorable. Out of spite a child can embrace sensuality, a false cult, or an independent spirit. That's why we as parents need to pray so much for our children, giving Satan no cause to plant seeds that will crop up as the years go by.

Like Noah and his son, there is a bond that ties us together. For good or evil, we are in the race of life together. I've heard people say, "If I do not attend church or if I embrace some sin, who cares?" But just because there is no visible bond between the children of God, that does not make a cause-effect relationship less real. When we stumble, we set moral laws into motion that inevitably lead to influencing others. Even secret sins have not-so-secret consequences. That's just the way God made it.

When Achan sinned in secret, the whole nation of Israel lost a battle and eventually he and his family were stoned. However unfair it may seem to us, God will not let us sin in isolation. This is particularly true of alcoholism. Studies have shown that the chances of children becoming alcoholics increase dramatically when one of the parents is victimized by drink. In fact, it may take a few generations to neutralize the effects of alcoholism in a family line.

If Noah had to learn how devastating the consequences of one sin can be, we had better learn the same lesson. No man lives unto himself and no man dies unto himself—and no man sins unto himself.

THE SIN OF FUTURE GENERATIONS

The string of consequences growing out of Noah's drunkenness does not end with Ham. God says in effect, "Ham, because of your attitude toward your father, your son Canaan will reproduce your rebellion. He is going to be cursed, and be a servant for all of his life. He is not going to follow the Lord."

Archeologists have verified this prediction. When they dug up the inscriptions of the Canaanites, they discovered them to be one of the most debased, sinful, and depraved people of all time. Every kind of iniquity known today was practiced by them, and the consequences were found in all their generations. That's why the Lord told Joshua to exterminate the Canaanites. That sounds far too severe, but the fact is that God was judging a nation that was consumed by wickedness. Since He had promised Noah that He would never again destroy the earth by a flood, He used war to rid Palestine of these wicked people. Whatever problems we may have with His judgments, let's learn an important lesson: God hates iniquity and every evil way. Though I expect to meet Ham in heaven, I doubt whether we will see many of his descendants.

When God says that He "visits the iniquity of the fathers on the children, on the third and fourth generation of those who hate Me" (Ex. 20:5, NASB), He means it. For example, Abraham lied to Pharaoh about Sarah. Isaac ended up in the same circumstances and told about his wife, Rebecca; Jacob ended up being a liar and had twelve sons, ten of whom deceived him with lies. There you have it: Four generations are affected because of the sin of one of the parents.

The Snare of Alcoholism

Of course, I don't mean to imply that the connection between father and son is unbreakable—God can reverse the consequences of our parents' or grandparents' sins if we repent. But there is a judgment that is passed on that carries with it a propensity to sin. Certainly this is true in the sins of the flesh such as drunkenness, alcoholism, gambling, and immorality.

Noah lived 350 years after this experience. That was long enough to begin to see the curse on Canaan take effect. Possibly he saw the results of that one act played out before his eyes on the stage of life. I'm sure Noah was restored into God's fellowship and forgiven, for he is included among the heroes of faith in Hebrews chapter 11. But the consequences of his sin were never erased on this earth.

If Satan has won a battle in your life, don't let him win a second battle—namely, feeling that it's too late for you to repent. He has two lies that he pawns off on gullible believers. The first is that one sin doesn't really matter. "Just do it once, and God will forgive you, and you can control the consequences."

Then when we have fallen, he comes up with a second lie, "You've blown it so badly there's no use standing up. In fact, if you receive forgiveness today you might commit the same sin tomorrow, so why bother?"

And once he has you there, he has a third lie too: "Now look what you've done. You've gone too far. You've committed too many sins and hurt too many people. Just learn to cope with your sins, but God doesn't want to hear from you any more; you're too wretched to be forgiven."

And when the devil has convinced you that there is no way back, you are stuck with the curse, and so are your children. But God wants to bring you back today so that He can minimize the consequences of sin you have already committed. He says to you, "I want to put My arms around you again. I will blot out your sin. You can walk before Me in purity and holiness."

When we read in Hebrews 7:25 that Jesus is "able to save to the uttermost them that come unto God by Him" (KJV), that word *uttermost* very probably refers to the person who is the least likely to ever be changed. It's a reference to Christ's ability to save those who are "hopeless cases." But the phrase "hopeless case" is a contradiction in the presence of Jesus Christ. No one is hopeless in the face of Christ who can touch those who are oppressed by demons and driven by passions.

Christ is still able to make an adulterer faithful, a thief honest, and a drunkard sober. If Noah fell into drunkenness, God certainly is not surprised that we would fall into some sin of the flesh.

But today is the day for repentance—for casting ourselves on God's mercy—so that the dominoes of sin might be stopped.

5

<u>GIDEON</u>

The Deception of Success

Have you ever watched the start of one of the big-city marathon races? Upward of 20,000 people crowd the street behind the starting line. After the gun sounds, it takes many minutes before the last runners reach the starting line. As the participants proceed down the course, the faster ones gradually get so far ahead they are all alone, while the slower ones never seem to get out of the crowd.

Getting in front of the crowd does not, however, guarantee you will win the race. In one North American marathon in 1983, a runner stumbled while nearing the finish line well ahead of the closest competitors. He lay stunned while a runner behind him passed by and crossed the finish line. The injured runner revived in time to stumble across in third place.

The Christian life is like that. Paul writes to the Galatians, "You were running a good race. Who cut in on you and kept you from obeying the truth?" (Gal. 5:7) They had started well but were about to leave the race because someone was distracting them from the finish line. In fact, it seemed that they had actually turned a different direction and were running toward a different goal.

One of the Old Testament's best-known heroes, Gideon,

dramatically illustrates that early success in the race of life may lead to dangerous self-deception, and in the end may result in a fall short of God's finish tape. Gideon clearly is a man we ought to study seriously.

Gideon grew up in an environment not designed to produce godliness. In his parent's backyard was an altar to Baal and a statue to Asherah, two gods from neighboring countries. Meanwhile, the land was overrun by Midianites, who were enslaving the Israelites.

Despite Gideon's pagan past, an angel of the Lord appeared to him and gave him marching orders. "Take the second bull from your father's herd, the one seven years old. Tear down your father's altar to Baal and cut down the Asherah pole beside it. Then build a proper kind of altar to the Lord your God on the top of this bluff. Using the wood of the Asherah pole that you cut down, offer the second bull as a burnt offering" (Jud. 6:25-26).

Afraid of the uproar his actions would cause, Gideon did it at night rather than in the daytime. Though a coward, he had taken his first decisive step of obedience. God honored that commitment and the Spirit of the Lord came upon Gideon and he summoned all of Israel to join him for an attack on the new invasion of the Midianites. As you know, God helped him shape that ungainly army of recruits into a fighting force of 300. The eventual victory was fantastic— they even captured the two leading kings in the alliance.

But it's after the victory that the temptations come. To his credit, Gideon did not become defiant or proud. But he was pushed into a temptation by his admirers; out of kindness he didn't have the strength to say no.

They told him, "Rule over us—you, your son, and your grandson—because you have saved us out of the hand of Midian" (8:22). Considering the ridicule he had taken from several villages in Israel, he is to be commended for not falling into such pride. He wisely recognized that it was not God's will for him to be king—God did not want a king for Israel at that time.

Yet Gideon fell into a related temptation. In the process he made a series of decisions that haunted the nation for years after he died. Though he meant well, he slid into an error that had far-reaching effects.

THE TEMPTATION OF A HIGHER POSITION

Gideon declined to be king but apparently felt obligated to help the people in a creative way. Looking around him he saw how corrupt the priesthood had become, and he may have said to God, "You know that something has to be done. I really cannot see myself as king, but I think I can handle the priesthood." So he goes ahead with what he thinks is a reasonable alternative.

Often we push a successful person into a position for which he/she is not qualified: The Peter Principle. We expect that because the person has been successful in one task, he or she is qualified to handle other responsibilities. We think that a successful pastor ought to become the president of a seminary or that an aggressive businessman will make a good elder. We need to firmly resist the temptation to push people beyond the limits of their God-given ability and calling.

Gideon was now taking a responsibility that was contrary to God's will. "I do have one request, that each of you give me an earring from your share of the plunder" (8:24), he told the people. They responded in obvious gratitude. Since they had just routed 135,000 Ishmaelites who wore earrings, the gold accumulated quickly. Calculated by today's price, the value would be in the neighborhood of $350,000.

Gideon wasn't greedy. The historian simply records, "Gideon made the gold into an ephod" (8:27). This was a garment shaped somewhat like an apron and worn by the high priest during worship in the tabernacle. Over it, the high priest wore a linen breast plate with two stones used to determine the will of God (see Ex. 28:1-14).

The Deception of Success

Gideon knew that the Lord was with him and therefore assumed that this ephod could help the nation. Unfortunately, he failed to obey God's explicit commands regarding the priesthood. Specifically, he had violated three commands. The first was that priests were to be from the family of Levites and only to come from the line of Aaron (Ex. 28). Since Gideon did not come from a Levitic family, he had no right to assume priestly duties.

Second, Gideon used the wrong material to make the Ephod. It was to be made of blue cloth, not gold. Of course, the people thought God would be pleased with the precious metal, but He prefers obedience to beauty.

Finally, Gideon placed the center of worship in Ophrah, his hometown. Yet God had clearly said that the tabernacle, the center of worship, was to be in Shiloh. So Gideon broke a third commandment.

Regardless of how corrupt the priesthood was, Gideon had no right to disregard God's instructions. No doubt he was sincere, but God does not accept excuses. Gideon's compromises seemed small, but they speedily aroused the displeasure of God.

The same is still true today. A young man may wish to marry a non-Christian girl; or he may compromise his morals for the sake of some immediate pleasure. Though the behavior can be rationalized, God does not excuse sin.

A businessman may say, "Look, you don't understand the business jungle. Competitors on my left and right are cheating. There's no way I can stay in business without compromising. If I were totally honest, the competition would drive me to bankruptcy."

But God cannot honor disobedience, regardless of how reasonable it seems to us. Even if our heart is in the right place, as Gideon's was, God does not bend the rules for having good intentions.

Gideon had taken the first step on a slippery slope. One sin would soon spawn others and eventually a whole generation would be affected.

THE TEMPTATION OF IDOLATRY

Once Gideon had set himself up as a high priest and placed the center of worship in his hometown, idolatry swiftly followed. The biblical account says starkly, "All Israel prostituted themselves by worshiping it [the ephod] there, and it became a snare to Gideon and his family" (Jud. 8:27).

Clearly, the gold ephod represented power to the ordinary citizen in Israel. God's warning against idolatry did not seem to be important to those whose hearts were set on a tangible representation of their faith.

Of course, Christianity can have its trappings too. There's nothing wrong with a beautiful church building, but for some it could be a stumbling block. They may think that God is impressed with stone, steel, and even crystal.

And what about relics venerated by some members of the Roman Catholic Church? My wife and I have been to churches in Italy. We've seen the chains that supposedly were used to shackle Peter and John when they were in prison and the basin Jesus is supposed to have used when He washed His disciples' feet. We saw people bow down before relics like these, thinking that somehow this would give them potential merit in the sight of God. Such objects have become a snare to many.

Gideon surely knew that the people were sinning, but he apparently did not lift up his voice or hand as the parade of worshipers approached the ephod. Maybe he even thought that God had made an exception for him.

There are many other forms of idolatry. Whenever we hug a sin to our bosom, we are admitting that there is something in our lives more important to us than God. Maybe it's lust, greed, or pride. Idolatry is whatever we hold back when God begins to search our hearts.

I remember hearing a missionary tell how people caught monkeys in a pagan culture, similar to a method used in one of Aesop's fables. They took a pumpkin, cut a hole in it perhaps the size of a fifty-cent piece. It was just large enough for a monkey's hand. Then they put all kinds of goodies in the pumpkin. The monkey would slip his hand through the hole, load up on goodies, and try to withdraw his hand. Naturally, his bulging hand wouldn't move through the hole. When the people approached, the monkey would frantically try to extract his hand. Though it meant getting caught, he refused to let go of his treasure. The treasure was more important than life itself.

What is in your hand? Maybe it's your dream—a marriage, career, acceptance by your family, or the admiration of your peers. Are you willing to let go for God? He may want to use you in a less conspicuous place and ministry. Are you willing to let go of your dream?

God hates the divided spirit that cannot focus on worshiping Him alone. And when we refuse to give Him everything that is in our hand and heart, we take one step farther away from Him into greater disobedience. For Gideon, the next step was sensual indulgence.

THE TEMPTATION OF SENSUAL FULFILMENT

The perks of leadership are many. It's the "I-deserve-it" syndrome. For Gideon the personal reward for leadership was a bevy of beauties: wives.

The Bible reports, "Jerub-Baal [a name his father gave Gideon after he destroyed Baal] the son of Joash went back home to live. He had 70 sons of his own, for he had many wives. His concubine, who lived in Shechem, also bore him a son, whom he named Abimelech" (Jud. 8:29-31).

In Gideon's day, as in ours, leadership meant having more than anyone else. His military prowess had established him as the young outstanding man of his day, and an abundance of wives seemed deserved. Yet God had explicitly forbidden "multiplying" wives (see Deuteronomy 17:17, KJV). This was particularly true of priests.

Gideon had given himself to a sensual lifestyle, and therefore he was not satisfied with himself or his private harem. He set up a concubine in the seat of power, She-chem. And she bore him a son. Of course, the term concu-bine is a social euphemism for mistress.

What happened as a result? Abimelech, the son of the concubine, got together a band of ruffians and killed every one of his seventy half brothers.

When will we learn that God does not make exceptions for religious leaders? When we begin to think we deserve some extras, our "Abimelech" may come back to haunt us. We cannot take shortcuts regarding moral purity and in-tegrity. Regardless of how much blessing God gives us when we compromise, eventually He will collect.

What happened after Gideon's death? "No sooner had Gideon died than the Israelites again prostituted them-selves to the Baals. They set up Baal-Berith as their god and did not remember the Lord their God, who had res-cued them from the hands of all their enemies on every side" (Jud. 8:33-34). When the lead runner makes a wrong turn, his followers go with him. The idolatry of Gideon becomes the idolatry of his descendants.

There is more. We read, "They also failed to show gratitude to the family of Jerub-Baal (that is Gideon) for all the good things he had done for them" (8:35). When you mislead your family, loyalty has a short memory. Resent-ment instead of thankfulness surfaces after the leader's death or fall from high office.

Gideon began life in a pagan home. Then God entered his life and he destroyed his family idols. *But in his old age he returned to the idols of his youth.* It's a phenomenon I've seen in the lives of many people: the sins of youth come back to haunt them in their old age.

That's why it's so important for young people to "remember your Creator in the days of your youth" (Ecc. 12:1). When we sow our wild oats their germination may take years. Eventually, the seeds will sprout.

The Russians have a parable that illustrates what hap-pens when we compromise with evil. A hunter was out in the woods when he met a bear. Accosting the man, the bear asked, "What do you want?" The hunter said, "I want a warm fur coat." The bear said, "Why that's fair enough. I, on the other hand, want a full stomach. Can't we talk about it and negotiate? Perhaps we can come up with a compromise."

Half an hour later the bear got up and ambled away. On the ground was the hunter's gun. As you stop to think of what happened, you realize that there was a compromise of sorts—the bear got his full stomach and the man got his warm fur coat!

Over and over again I talk to people who say, "Leave me alone. I can handle lust. I can handle alcohol and a little gambling now and then. I can even handle pornography because I know when to put on the brakes." But Gideon could not get away with compromise and neither can we.

The Christian life is not a 100-yard dash, but a cross-country run. It's not for those who want to become ninety-day wonders. Many begin well but end in disaster.

I've also noticed that future generations usually remember a person for the way he ended. Regardless of how successful he may be during his lifetime, if he ends badly, those are the lasting impressions that are left. As in the case of Gideon, they forgot his victories for the Lord and remembered only his idolatry and sensuality.

Backsliding can be halted, but we need to call on God in repentance and begin to walk in the power of His Holy Spirit. If we could speak to Gideon today, he would urge us to be fully obedient regardless of the cost. It's how the race ends and not how it begins that makes the big difference.

6
SAMSON

The Hidden Cost of Sensuality

Have you ever said to yourself, "There, I got away with it. Everyone said I'd get in trouble if I did it, but I've done it, and the Lord is still blessing me. I know He understands."

I've counseled men who yielded to the temptation of looking through pornographic magazines in airport news-stands, men and women entering marriage with a person who is not a Christian, persons continuing in a sexual relationship outside of marriage. Because God was not smiting them with judgment, they rationalized that He understood, and possibly even winked at their lifestyle.

The Bible tells the story of a man who seemed to get away with it for twenty years as a judge in Israel. He indulged in whatever his eyes found pleasant. His record of successes was so stunning that he had clearly convinced himself that he was unstoppable. And his peers seem to have cheered him on as a good man. However, the attitude of this man, Samson, was clearly the modern one, "If I like it, I'll do it!"

Several years ago I appeared on the Phil Donahue TV show to discuss the topic of lust. Most of those present were convinced that Jesus was a sadist who did little more than give us a guilt trip when He said, "But I say to you, that everyone who looks on a woman to lust for her has committed adultery with her already in his heart" (Matt. 5:28, NASB). Such a standard appears impossible. And, of course, the person of the world will not accept His drastic suggestions regarding how to deal with it.

Yet Samson's story reveals that when we are not willing to stand against lust, we will eventually be trapped and ruined by it. There is no sensation that promises so much, yet in the end stings so bitterly.

There is a certain poignancy about the news that a Christian worker is divorcing his wife for a secretary, or a national political figure confessing to an adulterous relationship even though he has a reputation for decrying the breakdown of today's family. Then there is the picture in our newspapers of a British cabinet minister stepping down because of an extramarital affair after a meteoric political career, and a Miss America who is stripped of her crown. Clearly, each believed for a time that he or she could get away with it.

Samson started his career as a judge in Israel with such daring that it must have been scarey to his parents. Talk about a candidate for MVP, president of his day's International Federation, entry to the All-World Hall of Fame. He had the physique of an Olympic athlete and the ready wit of a toastmaster. His ability to tell riddles astounded even Israel's enemies, the Philistines. What is more, he was a likable person.

Add to all these advantages the fact that Samson had been chosen by God to "begin the deliverance of Israel from the hands of the Philistines" (Jud. 13:5). A man of God who had the appearance of an angel had actually predicted his birth and his prominence, telling his parents to raise him as a person set apart for God, a Nazarite.

Historians have concluded that two things must come together for a person to become great. One is real ability, the other is the opportunity actually to prove it. Consider Sir Winston Churchill, whose considerable abilities went largely unnoticed until he was thrust into the limelight at the start of World War II.

Samson represents a similar combination of ability and opportunity. The nation Israel was experiencing a vacuum of leadership. There was a desperate need for someone who could fight the powerful, implacable foes of Israel, the Philistines. Samson filled a crucial role in leadership for twenty years. His feats of strength endeared him to the people. Though greatly admired by the Israelites, he would eventually become entangled by the cords of his own sin.

Martin Luther said that God allows Christian leaders to fall into immorality as a judgment on the sin of pride in their life. God is so jealous for His own glory that he will bring any man to shame who has grown conceited. Pride, Luther says, always precedes sexual sin.

Undoubtedly, this was true of Samson, the champion wrestler who became Samson the weakling; the fighter who slew 3,000 with the jawbone of an ass became a slave. The man who apparently could have any woman who pleased his eyes ended up grinding corn for the enemy. Because his eyes had been gouged out, he had to be guided to his seat at a national celebration.

What turned the cheers into jeers, the hero into the butt of jokes? I suggest it was *blindness*, the inability to look at life from God's point of view. He was blind spiritually, morally, and eventually physically.

SPIRITUAL BLINDNESS

The first step toward spiritual blindness is always disobedience. It's the mistaken notion that you know better than those in authority, whether your own parents or God. The Lord had specifically said that the Israelites were not to intermarry with pagans. Yet Samson decided he knew better.

The Bible is straightforward about the events: "Samson

The Hidden Cost of Sensuality

went down to Timnah and saw there a young Philistine woman. When he returned he said to his father and mother, 'I have seen a Philistine woman in Timnah; now, get her for me as my wife' " (Jud. 14:1-2). Samson's parents knew what God had said and tried to set him straight, but they proved as unsuccessful as most parents of sons or daughters who haven't gained spiritual sight. Samson's response could have come straight out of a family debate today, "Get her for me, for she looks good to me."

The marriage was doomed to failure. If most of us have astigmatism when we enter marriage, Samson must have had cataracts. How he expected a marriage made in disobedience to God to work is unclear—except that he was blind to the reality of his actions.

So Samson disobeyed his parents, the very ones who had received a message from God about him. Undoubtedly, they often rehearsed the story of the angel's appearance, of his startling message about a son who would deliver Israel from the Philistines, and about the importance of adhering to the Nazarite vow. As they kept wine from him and refused to cut his hair, they must have shared the reason with him. Yet when his parents asked, "Why get a woman from the uncircumcised neighbors?" Samson tersely replied, "Get her for me. She's the right one for me" (Jud. 14:3). It was willful disobedience.

With his parents in tow, Samson hosted a wedding feast. He told a riddle about getting honey from the lion he had slain, but no one guessed what he was talking about. Rather than be humiliated by this brash young Israelite, the Philistine guests blackmailed his new bride into getting the secret of the riddle. "You don't really love me," she repeated again and again until Samson finally yielded to her plea and told her the hidden meaning of the riddle.

God, according to Judges 14:19, turned the incident into an opportunity to weaken the Philistines. Samson had said that if anyone told him the meaning of the riddle, he would give them thirty changes of clothes. So he went down to

---

Ashkelon and struck down thirty men to acquire the suits he needed to fulfill his promise.

Obviously angry at his wife for her collaboration with the Philistines in forcing him to reveal the secret of his riddle, Samson went home to his father. During his absence his wife was given to the best man at the wedding. When Samson returned, he received short shrift from his would-be father-in-law and was refused access to see his ex-wife. Thoroughly angry, Samson caught 300 foxes, tied their tails together in pairs, attached burning torches, and turned them loose in the standing grain. The resulting fire spread to both the vineyards and the olive groves of the Philistines. In retaliation, the Philistines burned the young woman and her father in another torching. Again Samson retaliated with a massacre of the Philistines.

Samson's massacre of dozens of the Philistines established him as their Public Enemy No. 1. Yet when they attempted to kill him, he killed another 3,000 Philistines. Clearly, he was a man of superhuman strength.

At this point, Samson's self-confidence increased. I can just imagine him saying to himself, "You see! I can do as I please and the Spirit of the Lord God is still upon me." He could disobey his parents, retaliate with vicious anger, and yet God was with him.

Possibly one of the greatest incentives to continue in sin is the realization that God does not seem to be in a hurry to execute judgment. Solomon wrote, "When the sentence for a crime is not quickly carried out, the hearts of the people are filled with schemes to do wrong" (Ecc. 8:11). Samson had disobeyed God, but God's blessing was not withheld, at least not yet. A minister who became involved in adultery said that the greatest shock to him was that God continued to bless his ministry despite his continuing sin. "It was contrary to everything I had been taught," he commented. And because the blessing flowed, it seemed as if he could continue in his rebellion. Eventually, of course, God stepped in.

The Hidden Cost of Sensuality

MORAL BLINDNESS

If disobedience made Samson spiritually blind, then it was loyalty to his passion that made him morally blind. The writer of Judges reports as follows: "One day Samson went to Gaza, where he saw a prostitute. He went in to spend the night with her" (Jud. 16:1). A look was all Samson needed for lust to gain control.

When the men of Gaza surrounded the city to trap Samson, he walked off with the gates of the city. This was proof in his mind that the warnings of his parents and the commandments of God didn't apply to him. To him, it seemed as if God was with him regardless of what he did.

Of course, uncontrolled sin always becomes stronger, never weaker. When you give in to temptation, it always gains in strength the next time around. When Samson met the harlot, he may have thought, "If I can just satisfy myself this time, that will be it." But, of course, it led him into more sensual sin. He was planting seed that would bear fruit long into the future. There is always a span of time between planting and harvesting.

Since only repentance can break the downward spiral of sin, Samson, who wasn't about to submit to God, was now in love with another woman who would eventually lead him to ruin. Like many women who are well aware of their ability to seduce a man, Delilah knew that she was the key to Samson's downfall. The Philistines quickly recognized the street value of this woman. She was a superstar and was paid accordingly. After all, she clearly had the manipulative ability to deliver Samson into their hands, devoid of his superhuman strength.

How would you have liked to have been Delilah's agent? The rulers of the Philistines would have fawned over you, promising your client twenty-eight pounds of silver. All kinds of special favors were implied if only she would entice Samson into sharing the secret of his strength. This was life in the big leagues! Delilah signed—and if you were her agent you would be rich and famous.

Then the fun began. The manipulation occurred in four stages. At first, Samson was in control. Three times Delilah coaxed him into telling the secret of his strength, and three times he handed out false information under the guise of "telling all." But whether they tied him with seven fresh thongs or with new ropes, he was able to get free easily.

His third lie was more interesting. "If you weave the seven braids of my head into the fabric on the loom and tighten it with the pin, I'll become as weak as any other man" (16:14). Yes, this was a lie, but notice that he was beginning to succumb to Delilah's caresses. The very fact that he was willing to mention his hair showed that Samson was beginning to weaken. So far, however, Samson seemed to know how to say no.

One of the deceptions of sin is that when it begins to grow in our hearts it appears to be under control. If we are able to resist temptation, we run the risk of developing confidence in our own ability to handle it.

This leads us to the second stage in Samson's downfall: he did not run from the temptation but stayed in the vicinity of it. Satan is quite content to let us have a few victories as long as we hang around the enticement he puts in our path. He knows that if we do not run, he will eventually get us. It may take six months or two years, but he is willing to wait.

Samson thought he could say no on Delilah's lap, just like someone who thinks that he can continue to resist when surrounded by sensual temptations. Just because you can say no to the enticements of a woman today in itself does not guarantee that you will say no tomorrow. A Christian girl may date an unsaved fellow and resist his sexual advances, but there's a good chance that she will eventually give in; it's just a matter of time. If, like Samson, you stick around, Satan will eventually stick it to you. If you don't run away, your fall becomes almost as inevitable as arithmetic.

The Hidden Cost of Sensuality

The third step in the manipulation revealed Samson saying to himself, "I don't have to continue to put up with this constant nagging and the accusations that I do not love her. I'll tell her my secret; it will be just between us." And so like a young man who tells his girlfriend that if they go to bed together it will be just "their very own secret," Samson is blind to the trap that has been laid for him. Of course, he had torn a lion apart, carried the city gates up a hill, and killed 3,000 men with the jawbone of an ass. Yet the man who had laid out a lion now becomes the victim of a snake bite in the tall grass of self-indulgence. The bargain Samson thought he was getting proved to be a rip-off.

We live in a world of trade-offs. Consider the single person who thinks that a sexual relationship will relieve his desires and reduce the frustration level. Or the woman trapped at home by children and barely communicating with her busy executive husband and therefore beginning to live in a fantasy world stimulated by the modern soaps. "There is a whole world out there that I've never experienced," she says to herself. So she wants to experience the thrills and minimize the consequences. But unfortunately she discovers too late that the price is too high. She signs the contract and Satan fills in the terms later.

Samson's final stage of failure occurred after he had sinned with Delilah. Of course, he was expecting God to be with him just as He had been in times past. He awakened from his sleep and said, " 'I'll go out as before and shake myself free.' But he did not know that the Lord had left him" (Jud. 16:20). Though he felt as great as before, God had left his life.

Though the Holy Spirit doesn't leave us today as He did in the Old Testament, He is grieved when we sin and even more so when our heart becomes hard and indifferent.

Samson had mistaken God's patience for God's leniency. Of course, God was using this experience to teach Samson that we can never tolerate sin and think it is under control. Christ said, "I tell you the truth, everyone who sins is a slave to sin" (John 8:34). Many people think that they can back off from their sins if they just get real serious about it. In other words they are saying, "I am not yet the slave of sin." But Jesus tells us that sin always turns us into a slave. To commit sin means that we are out of control.

Years ago when Oliver Cromwell was lord protector of England, a circus performer came out of the imitation grass to do a snake act. He cracked a whip, and a huge snake came crawling out of the grass and began to wrap itself around the trainer until he was scarcely visible. The audience was ecstatic.

Suddenly in the stillness they heard bones cracking. To the horror of all those present, the snake had crushed its trainer. The man had lived with the snake for fourteen years, having purchased it when it was only seven inches long. At that time he could have crushed it between his thumb and forefinger. Instead, he trained it to serve him, but one day the snake made its owner the servant.

Sensual sin is like that. We cannot train it. We cannot negotiate with it or compromise. If we play with it at all, it will crush us in the end.

PHYSICAL BLINDNESS

Spiritually and morally, Samson was as blind as a bat. All that remained was the need for him now to be caught by the Philistines, who would make him physically blind as well. The record is curt: "Then the Philistines seized him, gouged out his eyes and took him down to Gaza. Binding him with bronze shackles, they set him to grinding in the prison" (Jud. 16:21).

Harsh though it may seem, it would have been better for Samson to have become physically blind earlier in his life, if that would have prevented his spiritual and moral blindness, than for him to have succumbed to sexual sin. Jesus was speaking about lust when He said, "If your right eye causes you to sin, gouge it out, and throw it away. It is

The Hidden Cost of Sensuality

---

better for you to lose one part of your body than for your whole body to be thrown into hell" (Matt. 5:29). To cut out your eye, painful though it is, is better than becoming victimized by an adulterous relationship. The eye and the hand are the two parts of the body used most in sexual arousal. Christ is telling us in the strongest possible terms that it is better to take drastic action than to fall into such sin.

Samson entered prison blind spiritually, morally, and physically. But while Samson was in prison, God began the process of restoration. At a national celebration we can just hear the crowds shout, "We want Samson! We want Samson!" They wanted him for ridicule and entertainment.

They had not realized that Samson's hair had begun to grow again while he was in prison. When Samson came out, he could not see where he was going, so he asked the boy who accompanied him to lead him to the pillars on which the building rested. There were about 3,000 men and women on the roof in addition to those who were in the building.

Samson then prayed—only the second time we read that he prayed—and he said, "O Sovereign Lord, remember me. O God, please strengthen me just once more, and let me with one blow get revenge on the Philistines for my two eyes" (Jud. 16:28). And with that he grasped the two middle pillars and braced himself against them, and with a closing gasp requested that he die with the Philistines. And the house fell on all the lords and all the people that were in it.

Samson reminds us that God often gives His people a second chance. When we fall, we can either fall backward or forward—that is, we can learn from what we have done and lay hold of the goodness of God. No one who falls is ever beyond the possibility of God's forgiveness. As his hair grew, so Samson's relationship with God grew as well. In prison, he finally came to his senses and was restored. Though he died physically blind, we can be quite sure that his spiritual and moral sight had been restored.

It has been said "that the bird with the broken wing will soar just as high again"; the implication is that when we repent of our sins we are restored to our former position. But this is not always the case. Restoration does not mean that we get our same job back, or that we have the same relationships as before. For example, Samson's hair grew back, but his eyes did not—a reminder that some consequences of sin are permanent. However, God is always willing to restore us to *some* position regardless of how far we've fallen.

The very fact that a person is alive is proof that God still has some purpose for him on this earth. He's waiting for the repentant person to learn his lessons, to be quiet before Him that he might be brought back to a position of usefulness.

7
<u>ASA</u>

The Failure of Compromise

Is it possible to compromise moral principles and still appear to have God's blessing?

Yes, it is. Not everything that is evil has immediate negative consequences. You can cut corners and be so successful you may think you are getting away with it. Let's list some moral compromises that sometimes result in outstanding benefits:

☐ As a car salesman, you can tell a lie and make a profitable deal.

☐ As a waitress, you can refuse to record your tips and cheat the IRS.

☐ You can falsify a few details on an application that will enable you to get a job.

☐ You can be living immorally and still appear to have God's blessing.

Failure is subtle. Its seeds are often difficult to detect. Often they lie dormant for many years, but eventually they will bear their bitter fruit.

What causes us to compromise? Often it is the difficult situation facing us. We succumb to the pressure of the moment and compromise our principles for some immediate benefit.

The Failure of Compromise

A well-known Christian businessman's publishing enterprise grew rapidly. He attributed the rapid growth to God's blessing because he lived by the principles of God's Word. But one day when sales dipped, he began to secretly cut back on employee benefits. He became harsh and demanding, venting his anger on them. He tried to cheat his suppliers and failed to record all his earnings. To entrust his business to God appeared to be too risky. Better to take matters into his own hands and make it a success. Pressure produced compromise; compromise created guilt, which in turn led to strained employee relationships and a sour marriage. Too often we tend to compromise when we are in a tight place.

One of the truly good kings of the nation Judah experienced a similar pressure. Asa, whose story may be found in 2 Chronicles 14–16, was the third king of Judah. He came to the throne with everything seemingly against him. He had a wicked father, King Abijah, and a mother who was so evil he had her deposed as queen mother because she made an image that encouraged idolatry. Yet Asa followed the Lord successfully for thirty-six years. He reminds us that we can rise above our background; we can choose to follow righteousness.

Asa, however, stumbled on the home stretch. He was a good man who fell but stubbornly refused to repent of his compromise and submit to God's discipline. He died bloody but unbowed.

ASA SERVED GOD WHOLEHEARTEDLY

We all love to see a man who serves the Lord with a whole heart. Reading chapters 14 and 15 of 2 Chronicles is pure delight, for Asa seemed to do all the right things and make all the right moves. He succeeded when a faint-hearted man would have failed abysmally.

You see, when Asa came to the throne of Judah, idolatry was flourishing. The people had become impatient with

prayer and waiting on God. They were only three generations removed from the manifestation of God's glory in the
temple, but already they insisted on a deity they could see
and touch. As a result they built altars on the hills to
worship the stars and pagan gods.

Asa, young man that he was, knew that one cannot plant
a garden without uprooting the weeds. So he tore down
these sacred pillars and asked the people to seek the Lord.
Consider the biblical record of his actions: "He removed
the detestable idols from the whole land of Judah and
Benjamin and from the towns he had captured in the hills
of Ephraim" (2 Chron. 15:8). He saw idolatry for what it
was and he did everything he could to uproot it.

Today we have different forms of idolatry: horoscopes,
Ouija Boards, and other occult practices are but a few of
the modern forms of idolatry. Even Christians sometimes
grow weary of trying to get God's attention. Why not have
a religion that promises direct guidance and guarantees
immediate results?

Asa understood that God hates all forms of idolatry: He
is not in competition with other gods. Seeking His will may
be difficult, but it is the only way we can come to the truth.

Political success followed such clear obedience to God's
Law. During his reign a huge Ethiopian army came against
him. Although Asa was greatly outnumbered, he relied
totally on the Lord. Listen to his prayer: "Lord, there is no
one like You to help the powerless against the mighty.
Help us, O Lord our God, for we rely on You, and in Your
name we have come against this vast army. O Lord, You
are our God; do not let man prevail against You" (14:11).

The result? "The Lord struck down the Cushites before
Asa and Judah. The Cushites fled, and Asa and his army
pursued them as far as Gerar" (14:12).

What a reminder that a ruler's spiritual perspective can
influence the outcome of a military battle. God Himself
fought for Asa because he made God the undisputed ruler
of his nation.

The Failure of Compromise

Unfortunately, there was also a period in his life where Asa disappointed God.

ASA FOLLOWED HALFHEARTEDLY

For thirty-six years Asa had followed the Lord with his whole heart. God had prospered him and the nation grew politically and spiritually. Then one incident caused him to stumble.

Consider the circumstances. Asa ruled over Judah in Jerusalem. To the north lay Israel, ruled by Baasha. Even though both countries represented the same origins, they were now enemies. Baasha decided to embark on military adventurism. For years he seems to have carried on border attacks on Judah, but there appears to still have been travel between the two countries. Apparently, relatives could visit each other, and those who insisted on worshiping in Jerusalem were let through. But one day Baasha decided to fortify the key border town through which the people passed to stop the traffic south. No more trade and no more travel to worship in Jerusalem.

If we can judge human behavior by previous actions, we would expect Asa to turn to the Lord and ask Him for wisdom and deliverance. He did nothing of the kind. Perhaps he thought the problem was so small he could handle it by exercising some political shrewdness. Maybe this came at a time when Asa was experiencing discouragement, and he wondered about getting direction from the Lord.

Like most of us, Asa panicked in what appeared to be a tight spot. He wanted an immediate solution, like we often do. Dependence upon the Lord often is time-consuming. On top of that God does not always do things the way we think He should. So Asa decided to push ahead without consulting the God he had come to know and serve.

I also have to wonder if Asa may actually have come to a point where he questioned God's ability to get him out of his predicament. Yes, he had seen God work—he had exhibited faith in God on a grand scale at one time. Yet as Spurgeon wrote, "The greatest faith of yesterday will not give us confidence for today, unless the fresh springs which are in God shall overflow again."

Whatever the reason for Asa's action, he did the wrong thing. His response is so contemporary you would think it was recorded in the latest issue of *Time* magazine.

Here's what happened. Asa made contact with one of his nation's greatest enemies, Benhadad, the king of Syria. Sending messengers to Damascus, Asa proposed:

—that Benhadad break his treaty with Israel and make a new treaty with him;

—that Benhadad attack Israel so that the nation would be surprised and retreat from newly fortified Ramah.

—that to make the deal palatable, Asa would give Benhadad silver and gold from the temple, the house of God.

The proposals were accepted.

Let's analyze the situation a bit. Good King Asa, the man who had supervised the destruction of idols, counseled a heathen king to break a treaty. Then he took the treasure from the house of the Lord and gave it to this heathen king. He robbed God in the process of carrying out what seemed like a shrewd political move.

Does this ever happen today? Does a spiritual leader ever decide to outflank the enemy by making an alliance with other forces in the community or the nation? Does he share his resources, gained from the people of God in good faith for Christian outreach, with his new allies in the attempt to outmaneuver the enemy?

In Asa's case, Benhadad was only too glad to oblige. After all, a little territorial aggrandizement was in his best interest as well. So he sent his commanders against the cities of Israel. When Baasha heard about it, he and his troops left Ramah in a big hurry. Asa assembled a huge workforce and physically removed the stones used to build the fortifications. He reinforced two of his own cities with

The Failure of Compromise

the stones from Ramah. At last he could live in peace, having removed the immediate threat.

Did the king's compromise work? Yes, it clearly did. Politically, Asa had made a smart move, succeeding brilliantly. No doubt the people of Judah rallied around him, for he had shrewdly removed the threat to peace and safety.

Perhaps this is the greatest deception of compromise. *It works!* Asa got what he wanted and the people were satisfied. There was only one problem: God was not pleased.

Within the evangelical camp itself, there is a growing trend toward accommodation—a feeling that we can select whatever we like from the Bible and leave the rest. We've been so caught up with the spirit of our age that, like a chameleon, we change colors to blend in with the latest worldly hue. When the gay rights activists argue that homosexuality is but an alternate "sexual preference," we find certain evangelicals writing books agreeing. They say the Bible doesn't really condemn homosexuality after all. They reason that passages in the Old Testament are a part of the law that doesn't apply today, and Paul was only condemning those who turned to homosexuality, not those who grew up that way. When the feminists press their demands for equality, some preachers have "restudied" the New Testament only to discover that Paul didn't really mean what he wrote—the husband is not the head of the wife, and women do have the right to have positions of authority within the church. Or even more frightening is the conclusion of one evangelical that Paul was just plain wrong. When a pro-socialistic mood sweeps the country, we have Christians who advocate the application of a Marxist theory for the redistribution of wealth. And if the peace movement gains momentum, some evangelicals jump on that bandwagon too.

This is not to deny that we must constantly rethink our understanding of the Bible and its relationship to modern issues. But if we accommodate the Scriptures to whatever wind happens to be blowing, we will become so absorbed by our culture that we will have nothing to say to it. In our zeal to be relevant, we will have all but lost our prophetic voice. I'm reminded of the boy who bought a canary and decided to put it in the same cage with a sparrow, hoping that the sparrow would learn to sing like the canary. After three days he shook his head in disgust. "The sparrow does not sound like the canary; the canary sounds just like the sparrow!"

The Bible does not leave us in doubt about the results in Asa's case. The Lord sent the Prophet Hanani to Asa to tell him, "Because you relied on the king of Aram and not on the Lord your God, the army of the king of Aram has escaped from your hand. Were not the Cushites and Libyans a mighty army with great numbers of chariots and horsemen? Yet when you relied on the Lord, He delivered them into your hand. For the eyes of the Lord range throughout the earth to strengthen those whose hearts are fully committed to Him. You have done a foolish thing, and from now on you will be at war" (2 Chron. 16:7-9).

Such is the irony of compromise. Though it is profitable in the short run, over the long haul compromise only strengthens the enemy. Regardless of how shrewdly we try to strike a deal, we eventually are taken in by our enemy.

Telling a lie might enable a car salesman to earn more money now, but by taking sides with Satan, who is a liar from the beginning, such a salesman is actually strengthening the devil's right to have more and more of his life. Every time we make a doctrinal compromise, the enemies of Christianity are strengthened. Whenever we compromise, we are put into our enemy's territory and weakened for future battles.

Let's not be deceived by immediate results. Remember when God asked Moses to speak to the rock and he in anger smote it instead? Water did flow. The thirsty people were satisfied. Everyone thought Moses was a hero, but in the end he had to pay for his sin. God told him that he could not see the land into which he was to lead the people because of his disobedience. Another leader would do that.

Do not be deceived by the results following compromise. God will have the last word. *Compromise wins games but it loses tournaments.*

How did Asa respond to the Prophet Hanani's message from Jehovah? Unfortunately, he didn't repent. In fact, he became bitter and revealed another side to him.

ASA'S STUBBORN HEART

Asa became angry when he was rebuked instead of turning to the Lord. He had the Prophet Hanani thrown into prison. When his subjects protested, Asa oppressed them as well. He had thought they would be grateful for bringing peace and now they sided with the troublemaker! Here was a clearly good man who would not admit to his sin even when it was pointed out to him by God's messenger.

See any parallels today? A Christian businessman panics when potential competition from another Christian develops unexpectedly. Instead of depending on the Lord to help him implement better business practices, he allies himself with ungodly men in the community to squeeze out the brother in Christ. When men in his company seek to alert him to the danger, he harasses them until they leave. Sometimes the move appears to succeed brilliantly, except that a brother in the Lord may have been destroyed financially in the process.

Why did Asa react so angrily? For one thing, he had invested a lot in his decision. It is hard to admit you are wrong when the majority is telling you how great you are. Clearly, it is not easy to change your mind when you have come from political suicide to political success by a shrewd move. Why should something that turned out so well suddenly be called a sin?

I have known men involved in moral sin who acted much like Asa when confronted with it. Instead of admitting their guilt, they found it difficult to own up to their behavior. Once we have invested time and effort into a decision, into a long-term choice, it is hard to go back.

Two men in government in Washington were reportedly guilty of sexual misconduct. One justified himself; the other admitted his shame and guilt, openly declaring that he was to be blamed. These two provided the contrast between a great man and a sinner who refuses to admit his sin. If there is one thing worse than the sin itself, it is the refusal to admit to the sin when it is pointed out to you.

Yes, Asa had invested his reputation in his decision, but he had also given the money from the house of the Lord to Syria as well. Perhaps he thought, "I paid good money for what we got, and I am not going to admit I was wrong." It is like the man who purchased a grossly overpriced house and could not admit he had been conned into a bad deal. We find it hard to back away when we have been taken for a ride financially.

Satan's strategy is to get us to make such a heavy investment in our decisions that we feel we cannot back out. He wants us to think that it is sometimes too late to back out. He reminds us to be unwavering in our commitment when we have set our sails in the wrong direction.

A young woman truly committed to the Lord let her heart be won by a young man who had clearly not broken with his past undesirable habits. He claimed to have made a decision for Christ, but his desire to fellowship was so weak he went to church only when she took him. The more time they spent together, the more the commitment to each other grew. Repeatedly, she turned down his proposal for marriage, but she continued seeing him. Eventually, the commitment in time and energy became so great she accepted his engagement ring.

Shortly thereafter, the young man returned to his former territory. He quickly engaged in old habits, making all kinds of excuses. And she made the excuses for him when confronted by her parents and family members. Her investment in time, energy, and money was at stake.

ASA'S DISEASE

God tried to get through to Asa in other ways than through His prophet. The historian reports, "In the thirty-ninth year of his reign Asa was afflicted with a disease in his feet. Though his disease was severe, even in his illness he did not seek help from the Lord, but only from the physicians" (16:12). Not that it is wrong to seek help from doctors, but the clear implication is that he sought the help of magicians. He was looking for those special cures that the godless people of his time sought. As far as we know he died without repenting.

The older we get the more difficult it is to repent. Every day that we postpone repentance makes it that much harder for us to admit who we are and what we have done. When you get off the main road, every mile you drive means you have a mile to come back. And as time goes on it is unlikely you will ever get back on the right track again.

The true test of a man is the way he reacts when he is in a tight place. Does he seek the Lord? Or does he turn to the quick fix, the easy solution? A river is crooked because it takes the path of least resistance. What a picture of the man who accepts compromise as a way of life. If we want to be straight, we must be willing to plow our way through mountains and not be sidetracked by the easy solutions to our predicaments. Only a man with firm convictions will stand the test.

We ought to pray that God will not cause our sins to prosper. We need to ask Him to show us the deceitfulness of compromise, despite its attractive immediate consequences. The Prophet Hanani said to Asa, "For the eyes of the Lord range throughout the earth to strengthen those whose hearts are fully committed to Him" (16:9). God is still looking for special men, for those who will not take the easy path but will do what is right even if it is more cumbersome, less efficient and, humanly speaking, more hazardous.

Though I cannot identify who said it, I agree whole-heartedly with this description of the man God uses:

Today the world is looking for men, men who are not for sale, honest, sound from center to circumference, true to the heart's core . . . men whose consciences are steady as a needle to the pole; men who will stand for right if heaven totters and the earth reels . . . men who can tell the truth and look the world right in the eye; men who neither brag nor run;
men who neither flag nor flinch;
men who can have courage without shouting it;
men in whom the courage of everlasting life still runs deep and strong;
men who know their message and tell it;
men who know their place and fill it;
men who know their business and attend to it;
men who will not lie; men who will not shirk,
men who will not dodge; men who are not too lazy to work;
men who are not too proud to be poor; men who are willing
to eat what they have earned and wear what they have paid for;
men who are not ashamed to say no with emphasis;
men who are not ashamed to say, "I cannot afford it."

8

<u>DEMAS</u>

In Love with the World

Soren Kierkegaard, that Danish theologian and philosopher, told the parable about a duck flying home toward northern Europe. En route, the duck landed in a foreign farmyard. As he looked about him, he thought to himself, "This is a good deal. This farmer provides corn and fresh water daily. What more can you ask?"

The wild duck also quickly became friends with the tame ducks in the farmyard. The environment proved so comfortable, however, that he stayed for a day, added another day (no hotel costs to worry about!), and soon he had stayed a whole week.

Once he had been there a week, it really was no big decision to stay a month. In fact, before he knew it the whole summer had passed—pleasantly, I might add.

In the fall when his family was flying south overhead, he thought to himself, "I ought to rejoin them." He began to flap his wings to fly, but he could get no higher than the eaves of the barn. So he said, "I think I will spend the winter here." And so he did. The next spring when the ducks were flying north again, something stirred within him and he thought, "You know, I'd like to join them." Now, however, he only flapped his wings. The next year

In Love with the World

when they came by there was no longer any stirring within his breast—he simply returned to the farmyard to eat the corn that had made him fat.

Sooner or later every Christian experiences the temptations of that duck. We are tempted to give up and settle into the comfortable lifestyle of those around us. We get tired of soaring, tired of the battle. We grow weary of temptation and say, "I've had enough and I want to rest in the world."

The Apostle Paul reveals a quite different attitude at the end of his life. In 2 Timothy 4 he recorded what appears to be his last message to his spiritual son, Timothy. He knew that martyrdom awaited him, and as he looked back over his life he wrote with confidence, "I have fought the good fight, I have finished the race, I have kept the faith" (2 Tim. 4:7). Then he looked forward with a clear note of triumph: "Now there is in store for me the crown of righteousness, which the Lord, the righteous Judge, will award to me on that day—and not only to me, but also to all who have longed for his appearing" (2 Tim. 4:8).

Paul looked back with triumph and confidence, and he looked to the future with the same sense of triumph and confidence. Yet when he looked around, someone was missing. He lamented, "For Demas, because he loved this world, has deserted me and has gone to Thessalonica" (2 Tim. 4:10).

Who is this Demas? We first come upon him in Colossians 4:14, where Paul sends the greetings of Demas to the Colossian church. He must have been well known in that church, for in his letter to Philemon, Paul again includes Demas in the group sending greetings, along with Mark, Luke, Aristarchus, all "fellow-workers." Clearly, Demas was in good standing.

Then the years pass and Paul was in his last imprisonment in Rome. Certain death awaited him. The glamor of travel and crowds listening to Paul's preaching was but a memory. There was no more basking in the glow of a leader broadly accepted and highly acclaimed in the church. It is as though Paul was hunkered in the trenches for the final assault of the enemy. And at that time Paul wrote those tragic words, "Demas . . . has deserted me." He had gone to Thessalonica.

Though the information we have about this tragic figure in New Testament history is limited, I believe we can learn three significant facts that have application to us today. We can see clearly that Demas loved this world, that he deliberately chose the world, and that he reaped the rewards of the world.

A CHANGE OF AFFECTION

The Apostle Paul is very clear about the change in affection in the case of Demas. He "loved this world" (2 Tim. 4:10). To indicate Demas' level of commitment to the world, Paul used the Greek term *agape*, the strongest word for the commitment of love to someone or something. It symbolizes the centrifugal force of a person's life. And when he used this word, Paul contrasted it with the believer's commitment to Christ's appearing, "to all who have loved His appearing" (2 Tim. 4:8, NASB), by using the same word, *agape*.

What are the implications of that statement? For one thing, we know it means that Demas let his passions control him, for we read in 1 John, "For everything in the world—the cravings of sinful man, the lust of his eyes and the boasting of what he has and does—comes not from the Father but from the world" (2:16). From this I assume that Paul's statement that Demas loved the world includes giving in to his passions. He was a good man who failed when temptation knocked at his door.

We know from the letter to Philemon that Demas had been with Paul in Rome. He had walked the streets and seen Rome in its heyday. As he moved about, he also saw the sensuality of the culture of that day. He may have thought to himself, "I do not like the repressive nature of Paul's teaching. He just does not want us to have any fun. He keeps emphasizing that we need to renounce ourselves. That may be fine for him, but I am young and have too much to live for." And "he loved this world."

Each of us has something within, the old nature, that responds to the sinful pleasures in the world and to the appearance of fulfillment that the world has to offer. Believe me, Satan is a master at producing glitter and glamor, which the believer should recognize as sugar-coated poison. Like Demas, we are, however, instinctively attracted to it, particularly when it is presented in soap-opera settings like "Dallas." We don't even have to walk the streets of a modern city; we can simply spend our time in front of the television set to have our passions, our desires, set aflame.

A BETTER CIRCLE OF FRIENDS

Not only did Demas love the good feelings when he gave in to his passions, he also loved the friendships the world offered. To him, these friends simply had so much more to offer than the Apostle Paul, the prisoner handcuffed to a guard. Just imagine yourself in Demas' sandals, totally identified with a man destined for execution. I doubt if many of us could handle the derision heaped on someone like Paul, and by association upon Demas. So we should not be surprised that as he left Paul one day he thought, "I've had it. I simply am not strong enough to handle the continued identification with a prisoner doomed to death. I've got a full life to live, and I simply must choose my friends better or I will never get ahead." And he simply kept on walking . . . walking . . . all the way to the ship that took him to Thessalonica.

Peer pressure is one of the strongest forces shaping a life, particularly during teen years. I was amused some time ago when I saw an article in a newspaper that the government was going to spend money on an educational campaign to try to keep young people from smoking. What a waste of money! A few may be influenced, true, but young people facing the pressures of self-identity are not going to be deterred by information that identifies smoking as harmful. Their peers tell them that smoking provides entry into the adult world, and that is all that matters. Young people I have counseled in my office have told me, "I hate this habit. The bits of tobacco in my mouth are so bitter, the cough I've developed so annoying, the headaches and sick feeling so distressing, but I do it because it is the price of acceptance." They buy the ticket that for them results in a place in the adult world.

As adults we have the same pressures. We succumb in other, more subtle ways.

If we are Christians, we may find ourselves in an environment where we would be laughed at if we mentioned Christ, so we keep silent. Maybe our boss, like some owners or coaches of sports teams, scoffs at Christians as "sissies." Hockey players, for example, have been traded to other teams because of their Christian testimony, so why chance it?

What is the condition of the person who loves the world? The Apostle John says rather pointedly, "Do not love the world or anything in the world. If anyone loves the world, the love of the Father is not in him" (1 John 2:15). Our relationship with God is clearly an exclusive one—no love of the world permitted. If we love the world, if it has our heart, the love of the Father is not in us. On the other hand, if the love of the Father is in us it squeezes out the love of the world. James identifies the problem and the cure when he writes, "You adulterous people, don't you know that friendship with the world is hatred toward God?" (James 4:4) If we think like the world, act like the world in our amusements, have the same habits, and have the same values, we do not love the Father, but spiritually are adulterers or adulteresses.

In Love with the World

If the truth were known, most of us have probably adopted the values of the world to a certain extent. For some of us seeing a scratch on our new car moves us a lot more emotionally than seeing a person who is doomed to hell. Others of us spend more time in amusements than in showing love to others and sharing the Good News of salvation in Christ. Quite possibly our goals in life start and end with ourselves, rather than being intent on fulfilling God's purpose in our life. If these are our attitudes, we love the world . . . and if that is the case, Jesus says, the love of the Father is not in us. We love the world.

A MATTER OF CHOICE

Clearly, Demas did not merely fall in love with the world. He had to deliberately choose the world, just like a young man or woman consciously chooses to associate with someone he or she loves. In Paul's case he obviously believed that Demas deliberately chose the world.

I sense that Paul wrote with obvious inner pain when he said, "Demas . . . has deserted me." What he is saying is, "Demas has left me in the lurch. He has walked out on me and my bonds. Like Lot, he has chosen the pleasant, well-watered plain."

The same is true of people today who know Christ as Saviour and then choose the world. They do it deliberately, though not without a lot of indecision and inner turmoil. Obviously, a lot of emotional pressure had built up in Demas, as it does in people today, before he defected. He had sorted out the alternatives, and Thessalonica clearly was the most attractive.

I am sure Paul had shared his vision of the future glory with Christ with Demas. Yet walking the streets of Rome he had decided, "I cannot wait. I want the glory now."

There is a certain amount of glory available now, as it was to Demas. Just watch the Academy Awards ceremony, the ceremonies after a team has won the Stanley Cup in hockey, or the World Series in baseball. Demas decided to go for the gusto despite evaluating the seen versus the unseen, the temporal versus the eternal, the future against the present, and he "loved this world."

I can just imagine Demas arguing with himself, "I think a bird in the hand is worth two in the bush. Paul is always talking about future glory, but who can guarantee that heaven is all that great? I will take my chances with the present, the world I can feel, touch, smell, and enjoy."

We must not overlook a factor that slows some of us down, as it probably slowed down Demas. Our relationships are important to us, particularly the respect of certain members of our families. Maybe it is a grandmother, an uncle or an aunt, dad or mom. In Demas' case it had to be the relationship he had developed with his mentor, the Apostle Paul. No doubt about it, Paul was not only a brilliant man, he also attracted quality associates and gave himself heavily to them. Even in prison Paul was a formidable force, a difficult person to walk out on, to desert.

I remember a mother who was leaving her children and her husband because she had begun to share her love with another man. I vividly recall the tears that coursed down her cheeks and fell on her coat. Tear after tear, but she left her family anyway. She had convinced herself that "I cannot take it anymore. Even if everything you say is true, if there is a heaven and there is a hell, I still choose the present."

A PROMINENT PLACE

Demas went to Thessalonica. Archeologists digging in the ruins of Thessalonica have come upon numerous lists. On one of the lists of prominent citizens is the name Demas. I do not know whether that is the Demas whom Paul wrote about, but let's suppose it is. Demas left the Apostle Paul and went to the beautiful city of Thessalonica, situated on a hill overlooking the Mediterranean Sea. Mountains ring it. In that city Demas ended up in the lap of luxury, having accepted the city's values, and became a member of the city council. He became somebody in this world. But what will Demas be in the world to come?

You may remember that Moses made the opposite choice. The Bible record reports that he considered the glory possible in this world and opted for seeing God who is invisible. He left the treasures and wealth of Egypt and was willing to live a life of derision and poverty because he endured as though he saw the invisible One. The issue was one of faith—and it is that today as well. Moses considered the unseen more important and even more real than the visible, intangible world. Demas did not. Do you?

A CASE FOR REWARD

The third fact about Demas is that he reaped the world. Now this is not stated explicitly in Paul's report on Demas, but elsewhere he made it plain that what a man sows he also reaps. So if you sow to the world, you reap the world. You sow to passions, you always reap passions. You sow to pride, and you reap more pride, until you develop such hardness of heart that there seems to be no way to get through to you. You sow to covetousness and it becomes such a part of your being that you will not give it up.

There is another dynamic in the law of sowing and reaping. Unless there has been a terrible drought, we always reap more than we sow. A farmer may expect up to forty bushels of wheat for every bushel sown. God also gives great increase as a normal part of our spiritual sowing.

I hear people say, "I am unfulfilled in the church. I have to find myself and see what I can do." They leave the church to grasp for fulfillment. It may surprise some, but God may well let that person gain fulfillment.

A Christian executive in a mission organization had made great contributions to the stability and growth of the mission. In fact, he probably was largely responsible for its survival during a critical financial crunch. Then he ran into a deadend. There just did not seem enough opportunity for him to feel truly fulfilled anymore, so he resigned.

A major company in the same city was only too glad to hire this bright young overachiever. They paid him handsomely to join them and promised him a bright future. He seemed to have the world by the tail, and God was letting him reap handsomely on what he had sowed. Then one day he sat down in the kitchen with his wife and said, "Dear, what in the world am I doing? I committed my life to service for Jesus Christ, and here I am working for dollars and recognition." He handed in his resignation without knowing where God might place him, knowing that God rewards our faith.

Today that executive is part of a team reaching the world for Jesus Christ. Over and over again, he faces challenges that would scare an ordinary person, yet he meets them and wins in the supernatural power of the Holy Spirit. He sowed commitment and God is providing the harvest.

At the same time I know people who have left the congregation I minister in and returned to the world who seem happy and fulfilled. They are still in rebellion to God's plan for their life, yet on the surface God is not punishing them in any way. But, of course, all we can see are the events of today and tomorrow; the Lord knows eternity.

Consider the statement that those who fulfill the lusts of the flesh will not inherit the Kingdom of God. I do not believe that Christians who revert to walking in the lusts of the flesh will not be saved. Inheriting the Kingdom has to do with ruling with Jesus Christ, not entrance into the Kingdom.

You will recall the parable Jesus told about the men who were given various talents by their lord before he went on a journey. Two invested their talents, but one buried it. The two who invested what their lord had given them were rewarded, but the one who buried his talent had it snatched away from him and given to another who already had rule over ten cities. Jesus says that is what is going to happen to some of us. If we sow to the flesh, we will be in heaven but have no leadership position, no cities in the world over which to exercise authority. That is the position in which Demas found himself.

In my counseling experience, I have found that when you seek fulfillment in the world you simply desire more fulfillment. If you feed your appetites, they grow and grow. If you live by your passions, their strength increases. When you sow wild oats, you always get more than you bargained for. Fortunately for some, they have parents who are praying for a crop failure.

D.L. Moody's favorite verse was, "The world and its desires pass away, but the man who does the will of God lives forever" (1 John 2:17). As a result he threw himself unreservedly into doing the will of God. He had his eye on eternity and its rewards.

A STRONG DESIRE

"But," you say to me, "I have such strong desires. I deserve some happiness, some fulfillment. I do not want to be gypped in this life."

Read the stories of Enoch, Abraham, Moses, Stephen, and Paul. I think you will find they were not robbed by God. In fact, He enriched them here and will vastly enrich their lives in eternity. I would rather be Abraham than Lot, Jacob than Esau, one of Jesus' disciples than the rich young ruler with all his possessions. Their faith helped them come to terms with the significance of the eternal compared to the present.

You may remember the story from the Arabian Nights of a boat on the ocean that was attracted to a certain position on the sea. The captain just let it go, taking the path of least resistance. What he did not know was that there was a magnetic island with tremendous power to attract iron and steel. As the ship neared the island, all of the nails were pulled out. At that point the ship fell apart and sank.

Sure, that's a fable, but what a point it makes. When we take the path of least resistance, when the world attracts us, when we fulfill our desires outside the will of God, we may find our life suddenly shipwrecked. Christian magazines are full of testimonies of people who set out to find pleasure and fulfillment, only to find themselves eating the husks that not even the pigs wanted to eat. Only when they turned to Jesus Christ for fulfillment did they find inner peace and satisfaction.

Surely, Demas had heard the words of Jesus, "But seek first His kingdom and His righteousness, and all these things will be given to you as well" (Matt. 6:33). The things we connive to get in an act of disobedience may come to us, but only to our ultimate hurt because they are not part of seeking God's righteousness.

I do not deny that the allure of the world is incredibly strong for many people. Demas did not desert Paul on a whim. But the attraction of the world can be blunted and replaced by the Holy Spirit working in us if we by an act of faith ask Him to. He is ready to help—all He needs is our invitation.

Granted, there are times when drastic measures must be taken. Jesus said that if an arm offends you, cut it off; if an eye offends, pluck it out. What He meant was to take command of the arm when it is reaching out for forbidden pleasure, to close our eyes to any lust-producing object. That sometimes calls for radical action.

We might compare it to a cancer patient going to a doctor and saying, "Doctor, I have a cancerous sore on my arm. Take out a little this week, and I'll be back next week so you can remove some more. One of these days you may remove it all." You know that is not what you would say. You want it totally removed, for even a little piece of

In Love with the World

cancerous tissue spreads its disease through the body.

The Bible uses a word that has fallen into disuse. The Apostle Paul challenged believers to "mortify those members which are upon the earth" (Col. 3:5, KJV). The translators for the *New International Version* use a more familiar phrase, "Put to death." The Puritans called this the mortification of the flesh, a concept we do not find acceptable anymore. It sounds too much like something a monk did hundreds of years ago before Luther discovered justification by faith. Yet it is a perfectly good concept, for we need to deal radically with those members that distract us from being the kind of disciples Jesus wants us to be.

Jesus wants you to fly again, to shed the poundage and apathy that keeps you in the world's farmyard instead of soaring to new heights with Christ. We have no indication that Demas ever dealt radically with his love for the world and its allurements. But you can, and you can begin right now by determining to seek first the Kingdom of God, giving Christ first place in your life, and letting the Holy Spirit lead you on the path everlasting.

And maybe you know a Demas. What should your attitude be? I believe we need to let our hearts be broken, like the Apostle Paul's heart was broken over the actions of Demas. You catch the sob in his voice as he says that "Demas, because he loved this world, has deserted me." I can say with confidence that Demas was on Paul's prayer list and was prayed for, probably on a daily basis. Instead of heaping condemnation on Demas, Paul expressed sorrow, leaving a note of warning in his comment. If you want to win your Demas, let him or her know that God still loves him and you are praying for him even as you disapprove of his actions. And what you sow, you will reap from the Lord of the harvest.

9

SOLOMON

Trapped by the Perks of Power

What happens to a good man when he gains power? When he comes into money? When he has the opportunity to satisfy the desires of his heart?

Maybe your mind has flipped to the story of Daniel and the three young men with him in Babylon. They determined in their hearts to serve God first, second, and third—even though anything they desired was within their grasp.

On the other hand, maybe you remembered Solomon writing: "I wanted to see what was worthwhile for men to do under heaven during the few days of their lives. I undertook great projects: I built houses for myself and planted vineyards. I made gardens and parks and planted all kinds of fruit trees in them. I made reservoirs to water groves of flourishing trees. I bought male and female slaves and had other slaves who were born in my house. I also owned more herds and flocks than anyone in Jerusalem before me. I amassed silver and gold for myself, and the treasure of kings and provinces. I acquired men and women singers, and a harem as well—the delights of the heart of man. I became greater by far than anyone in Jerusalem before me. In all this my wisdom stayed with

Trapped by the Perks of Power

me. I denied myself nothing my eyes desired; I refused my heart no pleasure" (Ecc. 2:3-10).

Yet what was Solomon's conclusion after evaluating his life of indulgence?

"Yet when I surveyed all that my hands had done and what I had toiled to achieve, everything was meaningless, a chasing after the wind; nothing was gained under the sun" (2:11).

Studying this king's life, I have to conclude that Solomon was the wisest fool who ever lived. He was wise because he was responsible for writing more than 3,000 proverbs and more than a thousand songs, but he was a fool because he ended up attempting to satisfy his sensual nature, bowing down to worship idols when God had personally spoken to him three times. The perks of power trapped him early in life and their vicelike grip on him all but incapacitated him spiritually late in life.

"The power of politics is very seductive," said Art Agnos, a member of the California Assembly. "So I keep things around here as symbols of who and what I am."

You can say the same about wealth, educational achievement, success in business. An American author and former business executive said recently in an interview that Japanese executives tend to have come through the ranks and remember where they came from. American executives in large corporations get so entranced with financial manipulation and the perks of power they lose touch with the workers, the producers.

You could say that about Solomon, who got off to a good start. His father had united the country, driven back the enemies on the borders, accumulated gold and silver for the temple God had said his son would build. The pretenders to the throne in the royal family had made a run at it, including Absalom, and been eliminated. So he started his rule as a king with the people at peace and the prospect of fulfilling his father's dream, the building of a temple for the worship of God that would bring glory to God and honor the skilled craftsmen given the assignment.

Yet Solomon had a special advantage for another reason. The biblical historian records, "Bathsheba . . . gave birth to a son, and they named him Solomon. The Lord loved him; and because the Lord loved him, He sent word through Nathan the prophet to name him Jedidiah" (2 Sam. 12:24-25). What a way to start your life in a royal household!

Yet in Solomon, the good man, there was always a mixture of evil that prevented him from achieving the status of an Abraham, a David, or even a Samuel. Iron and clay were mixed, and the result had a fatal flaw, a personality weakness if you will, that resulted in a crumbling of the moral will, even though he seemed to have everything going for him. Outwardly, he looked magnificent in his power and his kingdom's achievements, but the weakness was there and brought on the collapse of the empire in the very next generation.

Let's examine the entrapment of Solomon by the perks of power against the backdrop of God's three appearances to him. During the first appearance, God tested Solomon's heart. When He spoke to Solomon the second time, there was a strong note of warning. The third time God judged his heart and pronounced judgment on his family.

A TEST OF PURPOSE

Ever hear someone say, "Unless every sin is confessed, God will not hear your prayer or speak to you"? If that is the case, what do you make of the sequence of events in 1 Kings 3? Look at the first verse, "Solomon made an alliance with Pharaoh king of Egypt and married his daughter." How many commands of God did Solomon disobey in that one verse? Read Deuteronomy 17:17 and find out. Now look at 1 Kings 3:3: "He offered sacrifices and burnt incense on the high places." Another clear violation of God's command.

Trapped by the Perks of Power

In spite of these instances of disobedience that God records in His Word, "Solomon showed his love for the Lord by walking according the the statutes of his father David" (3:3). God apparently overlooked the examples of disobedience because he knew Solomon's heart was inclined to serving God. Yet that did not keep Solomon's disobedience from becoming the snare used to entrap him later. God's blessing despite disobedience does not mean that the sin will not become our downfall; it just demonstrates His long-suffering and loving-kindness to us.

More amazing than God's seeming unconcern about Solomon's disobedience is that God appears to Solomon with an astonishing proposition: "Ask for whatever you want Me to give you."

You may be saying to yourself as you read this, "God, You have got to be kidding. You are offering the world's largest box of candy to the man who has already proved he doesn't have self-discipline. Are You sure You are not appearing to the wrong man?"

We see quickly that God is absolutely serious; He is not pulling one of those "now-you-see-it, now-you-don't" tricks on Solomon. God simply says, "Ask for whatever you want Me to give you" (1 Kings 3:5). In effect God is saying, "Here is a blank check, Solomon. What you want you will receive."

How would you respond to a request like that from God? My children enjoyed reading the story of Midas, a character of Greek mythology. He wished that everything he touched would turn to gold, and his wish was granted by the god Dionysus. He had not thought through that request very well, however, for even his food turned to gold when he touched it, and the different parts of his body turned to gold as he touched them.

Solomon was wiser. He said, "I am only a little child and do not know how to carry out my duties." For that reason he continued, "So give Your servant a discerning heart to govern Your people and to distinguish between right and

wrong." What he was really asking for was wisdom.
God's response?

"Since you have asked for this and not for long life or wealth for yourself, nor have asked for the death of your enemies but for discernment in administering justice, I will do what you have asked. I will give you a wise and discerning heart" (3:12).

Then God became very generous with Solomon. He said, "Moreover, I will give you what you have not asked for—both riches and honor—so that in your lifetime you will have no equal among kings" (3:13). Many years later British Lord Chamberlain woke up an eighteen-year-old girl in Buckingham Palace, London, England, and told her she was now the Queen of England—and then read her this Bible passage. Queen Victoria never forgot it.

Did Solomon pass his test of purpose? Yes, he did, but the blue sky held a cloud the size of a man's hand, for we read that Solomon loved the Lord "except that he offered sacrifices and burned incense on the high places" (3:3). Incomplete obedience held seeds of destruction.

We need to understand Solomon. He was first and foremost a politician. The people worshiped at the high places, treating them somewhat like the local church. As king, he might have had an insurrection if he had wiped out all the high places—imagine doing away with the churches in America.

Solomon was concerned about the potential for trouble in another area, the friction between the house of David and the house of Saul. Determined to overcome that potential for civil strife, he set about to build a temple, hoping that the house of God would unite the family of Saul and the family of David. Every pastor knows that a construction project at the house of the Lord has a way of uniting the congregation. As far as he was concerned, Solomon needed to take the torn garment that was Israel and sew it together, bringing it under one roof in worship and royal leadership.

Trapped by the Perks of Power

Yet Solomon was not only a good domestic politician. In his determination to establish a great nation with stable borders, he embarked on what was common foreign policy in his day; he married the daughters of surrounding kings. After all, would you go to war with a nation where your daughter was a member of the royal court?

God had said, "I am going to give you a heart of wisdom," and He did. But in Solomon's attempts to play the part of the smart politician, he forgot that God was testing his heart.

A TEST OF OBEDIENCE

God then appeared to Solomon a second time. By now the huge temple with its incredible beauty had been built. After the seven years on the temple, he had built his own palace, which had taken thirteen years. Not that he had erected a large palace, but the number of laborers available were fewer. By this time, the temple had been dedicated.

Notice the magnificence of the celebration at the dedication of the temple. Imagine the priests sacrificing 22,000 cattle and 120,000 sheep and goats. The crowds must have been enormous to consume that much meat after it had been offered as a sacrifice.

You would expect God to respond after that kind of public worship. His appearance to Solomon is described in chapter nine, where God repeats a promise very similar to that made to Abraham, "If you walk before Me in integrity of heart and uprightness, as David your father did, and do all I command and observe My decrees and laws, I will establish your royal throne over Israel forever" (9:4-5).

Yet God also sees He needs to add a note of warning: "But if you or your sons turn away from Me and do not observe the commands and decrees I have given you and go off to serve other gods and worship them, then I will cut off Israel from the land I have given them" (9:6). Clearly,

Solomon had already married a goodly number of those foreign wives and this warning was needed.

By now you may have noticed that Solomon had a taste for the perks of power. The grandeur of the temple and of his palace, the number of animals killed at the dedication of the temple, all tip us off that Solomon had expensive tastes. And when we move into 1 Kings 10, we come upon an extensive description of the splendor of Solomon. Even today his accumulation of gold and silver boggles the mind. In fact, the historian reports that "the king made silver as common in Jerusalem as stones, and cedar as plentiful as sycamore-fig trees in the foothills" (10:27).

Solomon's love for luxury was only matched by his desire for women. What probably started as a little collection to enhance his foreign policy clearly became an obsession. The biblical record reveals, "King Solomon, however, loved many foreign women besides Pharaoh's daughter— Moabites, Ammonites, Edomites, Sidonians, and Hittites" (11:1). Sensuality made possible by his incredible wealth and power brought on the next step, idolatry.

Solomon proved the truth of the proverb that "there is no fool like an old fool," for we read of him: "As Solomon grew old, his wives turned his heart after other gods, and his heart was not fully devoted to the Lord his God as the heart of David his father had been" (11:4). What a classic understatement: "His heart was not fully devoted to the Lord." For in the next verse, we read, "He followed Ashtoreth, the goddess of the Sidonians, and Molech, the detestable god of the Ammonites."

A TEST OF REPENTANCE

What happens when you fail to heed God's warning? When the perks of power lead you into idolatry and sensuality? The experience of Solomon reveals the answers to those questions just as surely as it does the trail downhill into sin.

Trapped by the Perks of Power

God told Israel that He was a jealous God. With that as backdrop, read 1 Kings 11:9: "The Lord became angry with Solomon because his heart had turned away from the Lord, the God of Israel, who had appeared to him twice. Although he had forbidden Solomon to follow other gods, Solomon did not keep the Lord's command." Despite the personal attention of God, Solomon had gone after the perks of power, heeding foreign wives rather than God.

God pronounced a double judgment. The first is that the kingdom would be split: "I will most certainly tear the kingdom away from you and give it to one of your subordinates" (11:11). God would take away all but one tribe, giving the bulk of the kingdom to a rebel. In effect God said, "The garment you have wanted to sew together, the consolidation you sought, is going to be torn apart because of your sin."

As I read this I was so impressed by the fact that the judgment of God falls on the very achievement to which Solomon had sold his soul. If there was anything that Solomon had wanted, it was a united empire. His goal was to bring together the glory and the might of the kingdom, eliminating factions and external enemies. Yet God said in effect: "You wanted unity but I will give you disunity. You wanted a kingdom, and I will tear it away from your son."

God in his mercy did not bring this judgment into force during Solomon's lifetime "for the sake of David my servant and for the sake of Jerusalem, which I have chosen" (11:13). Yet Solomon did not get off scot-free. God's second judgment came during Solomon's last years as king in the form of harassment by an old enemy: "Then the Lord raised up against Solomon an adversary, Hadad the Edomite, from the royal line of Edom" (11:14).

Hadad had escaped a mopping-up operation by Joab after David had defeated the Edomites in battle, settling in Egypt much like Idi Amin settled in Saudi Arabia after his downfall in Uganda. Now with the support of the Egyptians, the very people whose favor Solomon had courted by marrying the daughter of the Pharaoh, Hadad began to harass Solomon.

On the northern border another adversary arose to harass Solomon. This time it was Rezon, who ruled in Aram "and was hostile to Israel." The message is clear that "God raised up against Solomon" these adversaries as a judgment on Solomon's unwillingness to repent for his sin.

If I could summarize the bottom line to Solomon's life, it would be simply this: *If success means more to you than God, then God will spoil your success.* He will make sure it rains on your parade because, you see, if you begin to compromise in order to be a success, God will see to it that the ax will fall precisely on the idol that caused your disobedience. God will spoil it. You will not be able to enjoy the perks of power.

I remember a man whose vision of success was money. Like many, he rationalized that it is a tough world out there. When you are in it, you have to meet the competition, and since everyone is doing a little bit of cheating, he did too. He cheated on his income tax. Some of the things he did could be paid for in cash so that no one would know how much he had earned. He would not need to fear government intervention. And sometimes he found that he could cheat a little on the quality of materials. He could say the materials were one quality and then deliver a different quality. He had it all worked out, for, remember, "everyone does it and this is a tough world."

Amazingly, God seemed to raise up adversaries right and left. The man had all kinds of trouble with the people he hired, running into one difficulty after another. God saw to it that success was hard, for when you make success your goal and disobey God, He will see to it that success turns into ashes in your mouth.

Consider the life of former President Richard Nixon. He had worked long and hard to achieve political power. Once in the oval office in Washington, he seemed to take a particular delight in the perks of power. Yet when he attempted to ensure his power and prestige by approving "dirty tricks" during an election campaign, God raised up adversaries against him. He lost all that he had gained and will go down in American history as a good man who got carried away by the perks of power.

Or if pleasure means more to you than God, He will see to it that your pleasure will be spoiled. I have seen people drift off into immorality, rebelling against God as they insisted, "Everybody does it." One day they find that the Lord has raised up adversaries and the pleasure they sought is tainted and marred.

This does not only apply to obvious sin. If marriage means more to you than doing the will of God, for example, or if some relationship means more to you than obedience to the Word of God, He will see to it that you pay for your disobedience. Remember, whenever success means more to us than God, God spoils that success.

I remember a man giving me a rationale for the sensuality he was involved in, and I couldn't help smiling inside as I listened. I remembered the words that "God raised up adversaries." What we are actually doing when we disobey God is inviting Him to discipline us. We are saying, "God, I am giving You a golden opportunity to step in, to intervene and smash my idols."

The Arabs have a parable that says that there was a worm secretly and silently eating away at the inside of the staff upon which Solomon was leaning. How true. God sends those little worms that somehow eat at our happiness when we are disobedient and refuse to repent of our sin.

THERE IS ALWAYS HOPE

Have you ever wondered why God did not just wipe Solomon off the map? Why did He go to all the trouble to raise up adversaries? Why bother with an unbeliever like Rehoboam to fulfill His judgment? It would have been so

---

much simpler to have let a servant kill Solomon.

The lesson I see in this is that God remains merciful to His children. You remember that Nathan the prophet came to David and said, "David, you are going to have a son and he will build the temple." And then Nathan added, "And if he disobeys me I will punish him with the rod of men." Those were the adversaries God raised up.

Nathan continued, however, and said, "But my love will never be taken away from him" (2 Sam. 7:15). So when Solomon forgot his commitment to God and sinned, God in effect said, "Solomon, you are disobedient; you are a backslider; you are trying to serve Me with two hearts; but I will not take away from you My mercy and loving-kindness."

Maybe you or someone you love is not walking in fellowship with God after earlier commitment to God and His service. I want you to see the encouragement that comes from God to you when He says, "My loving-kindness is outstretched to you. The issue of sin need no longer be a barrier because I have a remedy for your sin."

Many people think that God has His back turned to them. They come to Him and say, "O God, please change Your mind about me. I promise that I am going to do better. I promise that I am going to be a credit to You from now on. Lord, please, please." That is not the God of the Bible.

God has not turned His back on us. It is we who have our backs to Him. He has His arms outstretched to us. Because of the death of Jesus Christ on the cross, in which Jesus atoned for our sin and appeased the justice and judgment of God, God can now say to every one of us, "Return to Me and I will forgive you." The way has been paved for your entrance into fellowship with God again through confession of sin.

Solomon failed that test of repentance. If we went to his grave and looked for an epitaph, it might have two statements on it. One is, "His wives turned away his heart."

Trapped by the Perks of Power

And if we looked more closely, pushing away the grass, we would read in fine print, "But the loving-kindness of God was with him."

Today that same God says to those who may be walking away from God, "Come, enjoy again the warmth and comfort and love of the Father's home. My loving-kindness has not left you. The perks of the good life may have led you astray, but you now know they do not satisfy. Accept the forgiveness I offer as you confess your sin."

Right now you may be thinking of someone who needs that message. Let the Holy Spirit direct your steps as you share this good news with that friend or relative. God wants to use you as He did Nathan, even if the "Solomon" in your life does not repent immediately.

10

PETER

Overcoming Our Fears

What kind of salespeople have been at your door the past month? Let me guess.

Magazine salesperson.

Vacuum cleaner representative.

A carpenter looking for work.

A boy who wants to put you on his paper route.

What do all of them need in order to be successful? That's right, they must overcome the fear of men and women. You can tell by the way they present themselves whether they are free from this disease that can cripple their salesmanship.

Cult representatives who come to our door usually do so in twos. Usually the older caller talks; he's the pro, and the rookie is learning to overcome the resistance that they might encounter.

Perhaps you have participated in a door-to-door canvass of your neighborhood to discover unchurched families. Or maybe you have visited some of your Sunday School pupils. Have you ever knocked on a door hoping that no one would answer it? We've all felt that way because we don't enjoy the possibility of an uncomfortable confrontation.

Why is it that 90 percent of believers do not witness for

Overcoming Our Fears

Jesus Christ with aggressiveness and consistency? In a single word it is *fear*, the common desire to feel wanted rather than rejected.

Let's face it: there is a solid streak of the fear of man in all of us. The grocery store could sell us sour milk, and we'd rather dump it than talk to our grocer about it on our next visit. We would rather not tell our neighbor about Jesus Christ for fear of being thought of as fanatical. Yet, we can never witness effectively until we have overcome this fear. But we have a common friend in Peter, the disciple of our Lord. Despite the fact that he was chosen and trained by Christ as a fisher of men, Peter ended up denying that he even knew Jesus Christ, even cursing in the process! If you find it hard to share your faith because of what others think, you can identify with Peter's experience.

But what can account for such fear?

THE POWER OF SATAN

"Simon, Simon, behold, Satan has demanded permission to sift you like wheat; but I have prayed for you, that your faith may not fail; and you, when once you have turned again, strengthen your brothers" (Luke 22:31-32, NASB). With those words, Jesus Christ warned Peter about the trap that he was about to walk into. Satan was lying in wait to try to cause Peter to stumble.

In our day the devil is either ignored or made the focal point of attention. Though both extremes may be wrong, it's proper to study the biblical data in a balanced way. There's no doubt that there is a wicked, intelligent spirit with access to the human mind, and he is intent on destroying our witness for Christ. This evil being came to Christ to whom he is in subjection, and requested permission to put Peter through a severe test, hoping that he would fall below a passing grade. He wanted to put Peter through a sieve and prove that he was chaff.

To understand the figure of speech, we must remember that wheat has a protective coating around the grain called chaff. In Christ's day, this chaff was separated from the wheat when the mixture was thrown into the wind. Modern harvesting equipment uses a sieve, and Jesus was saying to Peter, "Satan wants to sift you and prove that you are nothing but chaff."

To many of us, a belief in Satan is a necessary requirement for orthodoxy, but it's hard to believe that he or one of his emissaries is always close by looking for a way to pull us away from God. Yet that is precisely what he does, hoping to put ideas into our minds that we think are our own. When Ananias and Sapphira told a white lie, they thought such deception was their idea. But Peter said, "Why hath Satan filled your heart to lie to the Holy Spirit?" The idea was Satan's, and he succeeded in getting these Christians to carry it out.

Thus Ananias and Sapphira would have found it difficult to believe that Satan had put deceit into their minds; similarly, Peter was blind to the wicked spirit that was intent on his downfall. Yet, every one of us goes through a sifting process. Think of the last time you were tempted; could Satan have been involved, hoping that your witness would be permanently ruined? Because Satan follows us around and knows our weaknesses, he cunningly plans for our downfall. Figuratively, he is like a snake, coiled and ready to spring at us to cause us to act contrary to our commitment to Jesus Christ. Possibly today Jesus is saying to you, "Satan has asked permission, and it has been granted to test you. When the temptation is over, I pray that your faith will not fail, but don't let regret over your failure destroy you because I am praying for you."

Yes, Satan can inject fear into the human heart. Above all, he wants to control our tongue, either in such a way that we will speak destructively of others (gossip) or, he wants us to be silent about our faith in Jesus Christ. His strategy is simple: he wants us to spread rumors that are

Overcoming Our Fears

bad but withhold truth that is good. This explains why some Christians can speak freely about politics, the World Series, or the weather; and yet they cannot open their mouths about the Good News of the Gospel. That paralysis can often be traced to the activity of Satan.

Peter fell into the trap of the devil. Though his fear seemed rational to him, he did not know that it had satanic origin.

SELF-CONFIDENCE

There's no doubt that Peter loved Jesus Christ, for he declared, "Lord, with You I am ready to go both to prison and to death!" (Luke 22:33) Let's not underestimate his courage in the midst of powerful opposition. On more than one occasion, Peter saw the crowds around Christ thin out and the number of true disciples decline. But though many of Christ's disciples withdrew, Peter, when given an opportunity to do the same, said, "Lord, to whom shall we go? You have words of eternal life. And we have believed and have come to know that You are the Holy One of God" (John 6:68-69, NASB).

Peter's promise seemed reasonable enough. He had been a member of the group Jesus chose for special training. When Jesus went into Jairus' home to heal his daughter, Peter, with James and John, was invited into the inner sanctum to be there when Jesus raised the little girl from the dead.

And who went up into the mountain when Jesus was transfigured? Yes, Peter, along with James and John. Peter felt so close to Jesus then that he assumed that the millennium had arrived—why not build a little motel where you can have Jesus, Moses, and Elijah as guests? This plan was interrupted by God Himself, who drowned out Peter's grandiose plans with the words, "This is My Son, whom I have chosen; listen to Him" (Luke 9:35).

Thus, Peter knew the powerful presence of Jesus Christ.

He thought he would never be afraid to take a stand with the Saviour. And there's no point in doubting his sincerity when he said he would be willing to die for Jesus.

Peter would have been a great encouragement to those who ask people to stand for dedication after a message on commitment. Peter certainly would have been willing to raise his hand, to stand up or sit down, to go to the front or go to the back—anything the preacher would direct. Yet Peter's commitment was fleshly even though unquestionably sincere.

To prove his point, Peter was ready to take on the temple guard when Christ's life was in danger. He drew his sword and missed his target by less than six inches, cutting off the ear of Malchus, the servant of the high priest. No doubt he thought that Jesus Christ was impressed and was willing to declare Peter a hero.

Have you ever made sincere promises that you later broke? Remember that you can keep no promises made to God except those made in total dependence upon Him. In a few hours Peter would be saying to himself, "Me and my big mouth! I'm constantly getting in deeper than I can handle. If only I didn't need to show off my commitment." You see, the bigger the promise, the harder the fall.

FOLLOWING AT A DISTANCE

After Jesus healed the ear of the high priest's servant, Peter knew he had made a mistake. Yet he did not want to wholly abandon Christ. To his everlasting credit, he was the only disciple who followed Christ at all on that fateful night. But his double-mindedness would soon catch up with him, for when you follow at a distance it's easy to become a victim of the many pitfalls along the way. There is no such thing as a stationary Christian life: either we follow ever more closely, or we drift farther behind. No one is strong enough to live the Christian life by keeping Christ at a distance.

Overcoming Our Fears

To stay on the circumference of Christian commitment is to lose the strength of the Holy Spirit in our witness. At best we can give Christ a halfhearted endorsement, the kind that would not make our neighbors believe that faith in Christ was absolutely essential. Halfheartedness makes the Gospel appear optional, a personal choice that is fine for one person but not necessarily for another. As James reminds us, a double-minded man is unstable in all his ways.

When Peter saw Jesus being led away, Peter finally realized that he held the "minority view" regarding the person of Christ. The crowds at best were convinced that Jesus was John the Baptist, Jeremiah, or one of the prophets. The religious leaders believed Christ was Beelzebub, the prince of demons.

Since Peter believed that Jesus was the Son of the living God, he probably thought that Christ would never be caught and killed. There would always be a way of escape just as Christ proved when they tried to throw Him over the brow of a hill in Nazareth. Peter knew he was with a superstar, who was able to meet the demands of every emergency.

But now, unbelievably, Christ was being led away and would spend the night in the small prison in the basement of the high priest's home. The powerful King of Israel was subject to humiliation and impending death. And if this would happen to the Messiah, what about Peter? He had no guarantee that he would survive the fallout. It's one thing to talk about bravery when you are standing next to the King; it's another when your King is led away and disgraced as a common criminal.

But there was more. Since he had tried to cut off the ear of the servant of the high priest, Peter knew he was a marked man. He could be easily identified and singled out for martyrdom. In fact, as he sat near the fire, he likely became aware of several pairs of eyes that looked remarkably like the ones that had seen him flailing his sword. If

Jesus was defenseless, so was Peter. If the Master would be led to death, the servant could hardly claim special privileges.

It's hard enough to share the Gospel when we are walking in step with Christ; it's practically impossible when we are walking far behind.

PETER WAS ALONE

Ironically, Peter became defensive when a servant girl recognized him and blurted out, "This man was with Him too." Peter replied, "Woman, I do not know Him." And when a second servant girl saw him, Peter again denied Christ, this time more vehemently; and when a third person tried to insist he belonged with the company of Jesus, Peter began to curse and swear, asserting, "I do not know the Man!" (Matt. 26:74, NASB) At that point, his break with Christ seemed complete.

Likely, Peter would not have denied Christ if John or James had been sitting next to him. Peer pressure is powerful, and Peter would not have wanted to lose face in the presence of his friends. To be sure, Christ was with him and even overheard his remarks. But Peter probably thought that Christ would die, and everything would come to an end. With his death seemingly sure, what difference did it all make? If Peter could lie and save his own neck, such cowardice seemed prudent.

Doubtless there is safety in numbers. It's when we are all alone that we are most vulnerable to temptation. To walk past a sensual movie theater is easy when you are in a town where your friends might see you, but it's harder when you are far from home in a big city, where anonymity is assured. It's the person who is alone who relaxes in the battle and drifts with the tide.

That's why wolves scatter sheep, to kill the loner; there's safety within the flock. But when you are cut off from others, the satanic attack can be more direct, more

Overcoming Our Fears

suited to your particular weaknesses, causing you to fall.

No person can live the Christian life on his own. All believers are a part of the body of Christ. The arm cannot act independently of the legs and eyes. There is, strictly speaking, no such thing as a loner in the body of Christ. There are those who help the body and those who hinder it, but no one is without influence. Peter might have been spared the humiliation of this denial if the other disciples had had the courage to walk with him to the palace of the high priest. But being on his own, Peter was not able to stand the strain of persecution. With a heart filled with satanic fear, Peter denied the Saviour to His face.

Because of the freedom that exists in this country, none of us would probably deny Christ with our lips. But we can also deny Him by our silence; our unwillingness to speak up when we have the opportunity means that we have capitulated to the fear of people. Like chocolate soldiers that melt in the heat of battle, so the silent Christian unwittingly takes the side of the enemy. If we are for Christ, we must proclaim it; if not, we have fallen into the trap of Satan.

THE WAY BACK

For three long days, Peter experienced depression and guilt. He would never forget the look of Jesus just as the cock crowed. The one who had said he would be willing to die for Christ was suddenly unwilling to admit that he even knew the accused Man. Fortunately, Peter was restored.

How did Peter overcome the memory of what he had done that dark night? First, he remembered that Christ had prayed for him. Jesus had addressed Peter as "Simon," using the name that refers to his humanity. At that moment, he was not Peter the rock, but Simon, the human being open to the temptation of Satan.

Why did Jesus pray for Peter? Was it because Peter held such a lofty position in the group? Hardly. Peter was the rash and egotistical one. He was not the mild-mannered, consistent follower. Christ prayed for Peter precisely because he was so weak, the kind of person who could be tripped up easily. Christ prays for those of us who are broken emotionally, those of us who have felt the crushing power of sin.

Furthermore, Christ understood Peter completely. When He predicted that Peter would deny Him three times before the cock would crow, Jesus was saying to Peter, "You are going to be scared to death to identify yourself with Me. But I know how weak you are; you will disappoint Me, but you will not surprise Me." You see, Jesus wanted to make it easy for Peter to come back. He wanted Peter to know that the hidden weaknesses revealed during the temptation were no surprise to Him. And He wants us to know that too.

Christ displayed a special interest in Peter's restoration. In Mark 16:7, when Jesus was speaking to the women who had come to the tomb, He said, "But go, tell His disciples and Peter." Just put yourself in the place of those women and imagine what was going on in their minds at that moment. They must have wondered why Jesus added the words *and Peter*. Why wouldn't they automatically tell Peter? After all, he was one of the disciples. But Jesus knew that Peter was not feeling that way. If you had asked him if he was one of Christ's disciples, he probably would have said, "No I am not!" But Jesus wanted to put His arms around Peter and say: "You fell, but you are not down. You have denied Me, but I am not finished with you. You have sinned, but you wept tears of repentance and you are forgiven. I love you, Peter."

Then, finally, Christ gave Peter an opportunity to confess his love three times (John 21:15-17). The third time Jesus asked, "Do you love Me?" Peter was grieved and disturbed, but he repeated his affirmation of love for the third time. Jesus accepted it and said, "Tend My sheep." With these new responsibilities, Jesus had restored Peter to his former position of leadership. Regret was replaced by responsibility, indicating full acceptance. The three denials were followed by three affirmations of love.

Outwardly, Peter and Judas did the same thing. Both were filled with regret, but Judas allowed his remorse to overwhelm him. Peter came back to the Saviour. Though Judas was pure chaff and Peter was a mixture of chaff and wheat, Christ proved to be pure wheat. Both were sifted that night and their true character was revealed.

Have you denied Christ by your silence? Or maybe you have denied Him verbally—either way, He's asking us to say no to satanic fear and yes to His promises of strength and courage. Later, Peter would preach the Gospel to thousands in Jerusalem, and tradition tells us that he died a martyr, crucified upside down because he did not consider himself worthy to die in the same physical position as Jesus Christ. Through the power of the Holy Spirit, he overcame the fear of people.

OVERCOMING OUR FEARS

Much is being written today on how to win our country to Jesus Christ. But there is a plan, which if it were implemented, could be used to win tens of thousands of men and women to Christ.

I challenge you to choose six non-Christians and begin to do everything within your power to win them to Christ. Two could be chosen from your neighborhood, two from your fellow employees, and two from your family or relatives. Then you should begin with intercessory prayer, asking not only that these will come to Christ but that you will have the wisdom to know how to unlock the doors to their lives. It's not just the end result that you want, but wisdom as to how the end can be achieved.

Of course, strategies may vary. For some it might be sharing a meal, lending a helping hand, or sacrificing in a time of need. For each, the means will be different, but

God will give us opportunities to share the content of the Gospel.

Your first reaction to this suggestion might be one of fear and unbelief; you're not convinced that these people would want to believe anyway. Besides you'd feel awkward.

If you have reacted negatively, it might well be that Satan is pulling the same trick on you as he did on Peter. He has injected fear into your heart, causing you to see all the reasons why you shouldn't witness rather than thinking of those reasons why you should. Actually, it's not a matter of your being able to draw people to Christ anyway. So it's not a matter of thinking that you are clever enough to win six people to Christ; your responsibility is to present the truth of the Gospel and then let Christ do the work. If He is lifted up, He will draw all men to Him.

If you aren't witnessing today because of fear, you are failing in an area in which God is waiting to help you. He will help you overcome Satan, a lack of confidence, and the distance that has built up in your relationship with Him. Then armed with God's promises and the prayers of God's people, you can help capture this generation for Jesus Christ.

11

<u>DAVID</u>

Dying with Regrets

What epitaph would you like to have on your tombstone? Enoch's was "He walked with God." Saul wrote his own epitaph when he said, "I have played the fool." Abraham's could read, "A friend of God." Christ said of Judas, "It would have been better if he had not been born."

What shall we say of David? However much he had come to worship God in his own soul, he was a failure as a husband, a father, and a leader. When the end came, everything around was falling apart. Many years earlier God had said of him, "He is a man after My own heart," but we shall see that David was far from perfect.

For a dismal portrait of a king who lost control and was dependent on his wife and good friends to save him from disaster, read 1 Kings chapter one. Only the quick action of Bathsheba and Nathan forestalled disaster. Take time to read this chapter as background for our consideration of David's successes and failures as husband, father, and leader.

DAVID'S FAMILY

How did David fare as a husband? Based on the evidence, he had a weakness for women, a bent toward sensuality.

Dying with Regrets

He could not be satisfied by one wife, apparently needing several to satisfy his passions.

David's first wife, Michal, the daughter of King Saul, ridiculed him for dancing as the ark was brought into Jerusalem. This public ridicule proved too much for David to handle, and he never had sexual relations with Michal again.

Then there was Abigail, who had made his blood run hot. She seemed exciting enough at first, but apparently soon lost her appeal.

One evening during the height of a war with one of Israel's perennial enemies, David caught a glimpse of a vision of loveliness. Instead of turning away quickly in the face of temptation, he appears to have gazed longingly at Bathsheba as she bathed on her rooftop in the evening sun. The text says simply, "He saw a woman bathing. The woman was very beautiful" (2 Sam. 11:2). While his physical eyes feasted on her, he closed his spiritual eyes to the devastation that could come from satisfying his awakened desire.

Aroused physical desire has a way of dulling our moral vision. Like David, we focus on the pleasure of the moment rather than the potential impact on those we love.

As David looked down on that rooftop, tomorrow did not matter. If he did not invite Bathsheba into the palace, he would always wonder what she was really like. Besides, he could probably get away with it. Swept along by the euphoria in his body, David sent a messenger to bring her to the palace, probably making up an excuse for wanting to meet her. One sin always leads to another unless we immediately ask forgiveness.

The affair was over as suddenly as it started—at least so it seemed, until word reached King David that Bathsheba was pregnant. Not surprisingly, Bathsheba reacted like all women pregnant after an affair: "The woman conceived and sent word to David, saying, 'I am pregnant' " (2 Sam. 11:5). In other words, "Now what are you going to do?"

There is no indication that David recognized the spider-web sin was spinning. He sent word to Joab, his trusted field general and personal friend, to send Bathsheba's husband, Uriah, home, hoping Uriah would be so anxious to be with his wife that he would make love to her and cover up the sin.

A man of character, Uriah refused to rush home and sleep with his wife. Instead, he slept at the door of the palace with the servants. He wasn't going to enjoy a visit with his wife while his fellow soldiers were fighting a war! Desperate, David invited Uriah in for dinner and served him so much wine that Uriah became drunk. Yet he still refused to go home.

Just imagine that Uriah had been willing to go home. Would David have been home free? Possibly not, for Bathsheba may not have been able to handle the guilt of her sin and may have confessed it to her husband. And if she had not confessed, she would have had to live a lie, pretending the child belonged to her husband. This could have produced so much guilt it could have put an impossible strain on the marriage. In addition, such guilt has a way of showing up as physical and emotional illness.

At this point David was still a man of action. He was understandably desperate, so rather than confess his sin he gave Uriah a note to take back to Joab, the leader of the army. Incredibly, the note said, "Put Uriah in the front line where the fighting is fiercest. Then withdraw from him so he will be struck down and die" (2 Sam. 11:15). David knew that Uriah could be trusted to take the letter to Joab without opening it.

Joab had no compunctions, as we saw in the way he killed Abner and later killed other rivals. He placed Uriah in the middle of the battle, where he was killed.

Did the cover-up work? On the surface, yes. But now the circle of those who knew of the affair had increased. Most important, God knew—and God took action.

Those of us counseling people see over and over again

the inevitable consequences of sin. God will not be mocked, the Bible says, and this is particularly evident with sexual sin. The very intimacy of it makes it seem so secret, but the effects are often so public.

David's biggest shock came with the appearance of Nathan and his tender story of a rich man stealing a poor man's lamb. Cornered, David confessed his sin, but in keeping with God's judgment, Bathsheba's child died. That was, however, only the beginning of David's woes as a father and family man.

Think, for example, of the impact of the news of David's affair on his other wives. True, moral standards were not evenly applied to all levels of society, and kings got away with a lot. Yet David's wives were undoubtedly deeply hurt, especially when a new first lady moved into the palace. Those wounds never healed.

If David made a mess of his life as a husband, how did he perform as a father? Badly. Very badly. Consider how his children turned out. One of his sons, Amnon, committed incest with his sister, Tamar. Absalom was killed by Joab, one of David's trusted military commanders, for initiating a revolt against his father's rule. Another of David's sons, Adonijah, coveted the throne and was executed. Though David had other sons and daughters, they deserved no mention in Scripture.

Clearly, however effective David had been as a military leader, he was an incredibly weak father. His sin with Bathsheba was probably to blame; he had lost his moral leadership. Paralyzed, he was unable to discipline his children.

Consider his response when his son Absalom killed Amnon for raping Tamar. David got angry with Absalom but would do nothing about it. The king even tore his clothes when the news reached him (2 Sam. 13:31), but he did not give orders to have Absalom brought to justice.

Then David foolishly gave Absalom permission to return to Jerusalem after the young man had run to Geshur.

Absalom should have been forced to stay there for one good reason—he had not given the slightest indication that he was repentant for the murder. Reconciliation must be based on forgiveness. You cannot pretend sin has been dealt with until there has been confession and restitution.

David was a vacillating father who did not know how to confront his children. Though we admire his compassion, it led to indecisive action. He gave the word that Absalom could return to Jerusalem, but he would not be permitted to see the king's face. Little wonder Absalom returned to capture the hearts of the people and had the courage to stage a revolt against his weak-willed father.

David treated his son Adonijah in the same way. When Adonijah exalted himself and aspired to kingship, the inspired biblical writer commented, "His father had never interfered with him by asking, 'Why do you behave as you do?' " (1 Kings 1:6) David, like Eli, saw his sons rebel but did not restrain them.

The only bright light among David's children was Solomon, whom the Lord loved. But even he had a divided heart. Sometimes he followed the Lord, but more often he turned toward sensuality. His loyalties were divided between God and the world. As David lay dying, the only member of his family who seems to have commanded his continued respect was Bathsheba, who told him about his son's revolt.

It has been said that a man should be judged by his children. If we use that measuring stick, David can at best be given a 2 or 3 on a scale of 1 to 10. As a father, he was a failure.

DAVID'S KINGDOM

By the end of his life, David's kingdom, like his family, was in disarray. Several base men were clamoring for his throne. Absalom had even tried to kill his own father to become king. He in turn was killed unceremoniously by Joab and his body buried in the Kidron Valley.

Dying with Regrets

Then Sheba, whom the Bible describes as a worthless fellow, revolted and galvanized the support of the northern tribes against David. No sooner was that revolt smothered than Adonijah tried to usurp the throne. Like vultures circling a dying animal, these men wanted to tear the kingdom apart. They had no loyalty to David; their only motivation was self-interest.

This can happen in Christian ministry when self-interest becomes the key motivation for top staff. Every man with a rapidly growing ministry attracts people who want to reach the top on the coattails of their leaders. One Christian leader confessed: "At one point I had to stop and analyze what was happening. I discovered my good friends and associates were all using my ability to raise money to fulfill their personal ambitions. Our ministry had lost focus as each built his own little empire as part of the larger ministry. When I announced we were returning to the central thrust of our ministry, they turned on me and attacked me."

That is what had happened to David as well. Ahithophel, David's close confidant for thirty-five years, sided with Absalom when he revolted. Ahithophel was the grandfather of Bathsheba, and he may have harbored resentment in his heart toward David for many years. David's military leader, Joab, supported Sheba when he revolted, switching to Adonijah when he tried to take the throne. Abiathar, David's personal priest for many years, changed loyalties as well. Surely David must have thought, "I deserve something better than this! Is this all I get after forty years of working hard as king?"

David had to learn, as many of us do, that life is not fair. Most people deserve better than they receive. I counseled a woman whose two daughters will have nothing to do with her, telling her, "Consider us dead." She has not seen them for twelve years. She told me she took the pictures she had of them and threw them in the garbage, hoping that she would be able to convince herself that she had never even had those two daughters. Try as she might, she could not get them out of her mind. Regardless of her mistakes, I think you will agree that she deserves better. Life is unfair!

David's kingdom was falling apart before his eyes. After he died it would be torn apart. If we are to judge David by the legacy he left in Jerusalem, once again we would have to give him a low grade.

DAVID'S HEART

What made David so special to God? Why is he even now honored so highly? The Bible clearly indicates the secret is that David had a heart that desired God. All through his failures he sought the Lord with a passion. In the end, he became broken and submissive to whatever God desired.

Consider the time David was told that his son Absalom had gathered enough support to ignite a revolt and capture the kingdom. David chose to flee from Jerusalem. As he did so, an entire entourage went with him. Zadok, along with some Levites, carried the ark of the covenant, hoping to keep it with the king. But David said, "Take the ark of God back into the city. If I find favor in the Lord's eyes, He will bring me back and let me see it and His dwelling place again. But if He says, 'I am not pleased with you,' then I am ready; let Him do to me whatever seems good to Him" (2 Sam. 15:25-26).

Surely no person could be more crushed before the Lord. He was willing to rest his case solely with God without retaliation and bitterness. That is the meaning of, "Let Him do to me whatever seems good to Him."

Later when Shimei cursed David and Abishai requested permission to take off his head, David responded with the same graciousness: "If he is cursing because the Lord said to him, 'Curse David,' who can ask, 'Why do you do this?' " (2 Sam. 16:10) David was now looking at life through the lens of a broken and submissive man. Though he could point to little that would be considered successful, at the end he was still walking with his God. Yes, he had sinned greatly, but he was a forgiven man. Tattered though his life was, he had seen the mercy and the lovingkindness of God.

There is more. God had promised David that He would make an everlasting covenant with him. Specifically, (1) David's name would be great; (2) he would have an eternal kingdom; and (3) one of his descendants would rule forever (2 Sam. 7:12-16).

How was this fulfilled? Remarkably, through Solomon, the son of Bathsheba! God took David's sin and wove it into the fabric of His purposes. The lineage of Jesus Christ was through Bathsheba and Solomon (Matt. 1:6).

One day some ink was accidentally spilled on a beautiful and expensive handkerchief. The mess was observed by an artist, who decided to make the best of the situation. So he drew a picture on the cloth and used the blotch of ink as part of the scenery. That's what God was doing for David. The mess of the past was being incorporated into the divine plan.

This explains the reason for David's greatness. Though trapped in a situation partly of his own making, but partly also because of the deceit of others, David could still turn to God. Though he was a failure in the eyes of those looking on from the outside, he could die successfully within because of the graciousness of God's forgiveness and the wonder of His grace.

DAVID'S GOD

To understand how David ended, remember how he began. In the hills of Judah, he first learned that sheep don't have to do anything to be accepted by the shepherd. They just have to be sheep. The more obedient they are to the shepherd, the better for them, because he watches and cares for them. A shepherd is responsible for his sheep. Visualize David sitting on a hilltop looking over a flock of sheep and writing, "The Lord is my shepherd; I shall not want. He maketh me to lie down in green pastures; He leadeth me beside the still waters." We want to interrupt him and say, "David, that sounds great, but the sun is shining, the water is cool, the grass is green, God is in heaven, and everything is right with the world. But, David, what do you do with your sin? What happens when you wander from that pathway? What happens when you commit sin and then murder a man to cover it up? And when you number the people when God says you're not supposed to—David, what happens *then?*

David continues, "He restoreth my soul; He leads me in paths of righteousness for His name's sake."

We want to say, "But, David, what do you do when your own friend, the only friend you ever had, Jonathan, what do you do when he is killed in battle? And what do you do when that little baby that Bathsheba bore you dies? What do you do when there is murder and incest in your own family? And when your own darling son Absalom is murdered by your own military officer? David, what do you do *then?*"

David continues, "Yea, though I walk through the valley of the shadow of death, I will fear no evil, for Thou art with me. Thy rod and Thy staff they comfort me."

"But, David what do you do when you're hunted by Saul and when you have advisers who suddenly follow a rival king? What do you do when you are chased like a dog through the Kidron Valley by your own son Absalom? What then, David?"

He replies, "You prepare a table for me in the presence of mine enemies; my cup runneth over."

Once more we say, "David, I don't think you understand, because you are dying! Just look at your family. Not a one has turned out decently. Just look at your kingdom; it's falling apart. Think of your wives, David, and what they think of you. . . . And now you're going to die. What now?"

Dying with Regrets

David replies, "Surely goodness and mercy shall follow me all the days of my life, and I will dwell in the house of the Lord forever." (Dialogue with David adapted from Norman Archer's book *David*, Christian Herald Books, pp. 142-143.)

We are glad David wrote Psalm 23 so that couples who have children who rebel, those who have squandered one opportunity after another, will know that God can still be their shepherd. Generations to come will say that they don't want David's failures, but they want his God.

And so the curtain closes just as it opened. All there is, is David—and his God.

What epitaph can we write across his life? The assessment that the Lord gave him in the Book of Revelation, "My servant David." That is all anyone could hope for.

12

<u>JUDAS</u>

Deceived into the Wrong Destination

An old Quaker put up a sign on a vacant piece of ground next to his house which read, "I will give this lot to anyone who is really satisfied." A wealthy farmer read it as he rode by and said to himself, "Since my friend is going to give this piece of land away, I might as well have it. I am rich; I have all I need, so I am well able to qualify."

He went up to the door and explained to the Quaker why he had come. "And art thou really satisfied?" asked the owner of the lot.

"Yes, I am," was the confident reply. "I have all I need and am well satisfied."

"Friend," said the other, "if thou art satisfied, what then do you want with my lot?"

It's a fact that few people are satisfied. Their desire for more will lead them into incredible sin. They will lie, become religious, or even betray their friends to get what they think will satisfy them. The disciples lived for three years with a man like that.

The name is Judas, not a very popular name today. I don't know any parents who have named their son Judas, though it is a name that frequently occurs on the pages of the New Testament. The last name is Iscariot, which

Deceived Into the Wrong Destination

literally means "a man from Kerioth," a town in southern Judah, an area known for its fruit farms.

Usually when we think of Judas Iscariot, we think of him only as an adult who betrayed Jesus Christ for thirty pieces of silver. We forget that he was also at one time a teenager, a young man with all of the idealism, fantasies, hopes, and dreams of youth. He was also at one time a baby held in his mother's arms, and he inspired great dreams in her heart.

Imagine the joy in that Jewish home when Judas was chosen as a disciple of Jesus Christ, Israel's bright new hope. No one could have predicted on that happy day the despair and gloom that would forever be associated with the name Judas.

Apparently, Judas was a man with great potential. His name is a translation of the Hebrew word *Judah*, which means "praise." Back in biblical times parents named their children according to what they wished their children to become. Perhaps Judas' parents named him after Judas Maccabaeus, one of the great heroes of then recent Jewish history. His parents may have hoped that someday their little boy would grow up to become someone people would praise. Every time they called him from play they would be reminded of the wonders and the beauty of a life lived for the glory of God.

His potential was demonstrated by the choice of Jesus, the faultless Son of God. When Jesus chose His disciples, Judas was one of the elite, the privileged few.

We do not know where Jesus and Judas met. Possibly it was when Jesus was in the southern part of the country. But after that night in prayer, Jesus chose Judas to be among those who would have the privilege of being next to Him, to learn, pray, and share their spiritual mission. Judas was not merely one of seventy, that larger group of disciples, but one of the inner circle. He had the privilege of seeing Jesus in intimate and personal moments. *Now at last I will be able to realize the fulfillment of the hopes and dreams I've had as a teenager. What an opportunity! What will the kids I played with think now? Wait until this gets into the college alumni paper: "Judas Iscariot has been selected by Jesus Christ to be part of His personal band of followers."* Perhaps that's what Judas was thinking. Unlike many whose dreams burst with the onslaught of reality, Judas seemed to have made it. His future was glowing and getting brighter day by day.

Yet, despite the potential which lay at his feet, Judas had some hidden flaws. These were not obvious to the rest of the disciples, but they eventually were brought to the surface when his true intentions were revealed.

HE HAD A COVETOUS HEART

Despite the good press Judas may have received back home, underneath his religious exterior lurked a deceitful mind. Though his friends did not detect it, the Bible lets us catch a glimpse of his heart in John 12.

Mary, Martha, and Lazarus were entertaining Jesus Christ when Mary walked in with a pint of pure nard, an expensive perfume. She poured it on Jesus' feet and wiped them with her hair. The fragrance filled the house. Yet Judas was somewhat less than pleased with this expression of gratitude. To him it seemed like a waste, so he pragmatically asked, "Why wasn't this perfume sold and the money given to the poor? It was worth a year's wages" (John 12:5).

Don't be misled to think that Judas had a big heart for the needy. He wasn't exactly concerned about the need of the poor. We read, "He did not say this because he cared about the poor but because he was a thief" (John 12:6). He was serving as a treasurer and pilfered from what was given for the support of Jesus and His disciples.

We've all wondered how Judas did it. Did he simply take the money because no one knew how much was in the treasury? Did he lie? If he was sent to buy food, did he say

Deceived Into the Wrong Destination

he spent $40 when really he spent $35?

What we do know is that in the close-knit atmosphere of Jesus' disciples, his covetousness came to the fore. He cunningly devised a scheme that apparently was not discovered until after Christ's death. Under the cloak of religion, he was displaying some of the basest attitudes and motives. He was living a lie.

Judas was a skilled hypocrite. Luke reports that when the disciples gathered together after the Ascension, the Apostle Peter commented that Judas had shared in their ministry. Evidently, he had all of the gifts, abilities, and powers granted the other disciples. When they cast out demons, Judas cast out demons. When they healed the sick, Judas healed the sick. When they preached a message, so did he—and the disciples never suspected that anything was wrong.

How was it possible for Judas to do such miracles if he was unconverted? Perhaps demons simply cooperated because they knew that Judas was a fake, and they were helping to hide his true identity. Undoubtedly, this happens today when those who are not born again perform exorcisms. There's no doubt that some people are actually helped and consequently deceived into believing that such religious fakes actually have the power of God at their disposal. Demons are quite happy to leave a person if they can perpetuate such deceptions.

At any rate, as far as the people who saw Judas were concerned, he was a successful confidant of Jesus. Whether he was able to perform miracles or not, the fact is that he fit in well with what was happening.

Let's remember that Judas was not the kind of person who slips into a church service late, sits in the back row, and then leaves during the benediction. No, he was discipled by Jesus. He would have volunteered to teach Sunday School; he might have been selected as an excellent deacon or elder, or even a pastor. He had the behavior of a saint, though he had the heart of a devil.

Nor was Judas offended by what Jesus said and did. He was not a troublemaker. He was more like a double agent who was consistently a part of all that Jesus was doing. "Even my close friend, whom I trusted, he who shared my bread, has lifted up his heel against me," wrote David in Psalm 41:9. Even though he wrote these words about his friend Ahithophel, they are quoted in the New Testament as applying to Judas, though the words *whom I trusted* are dropped, since Jesus, knowing his true character, never did trust Judas.

Despite his successful act, Judas allowed covetousness to grow like crabgrass in his heart. Though well concealed, it would soon be his downfall.

HE HAD A DECEITFUL MIND

When the heart is covetous, the mind must scheme to fulfill those desires. Judas had taken a special liking for silver, and when the high priests were searching for someone to betray Jesus, Judas grabbed at the chance.

In John 13 Jesus had just washed the disciples' feet. They were reclining at a table. Judas had already made the decision to betray Jesus, having gone to the high priest to find out how much He was worth. Thus Christ is stooping to wash the feet of the man who had already made plans to betray Him.

According to custom, they were gathered for the Feast of Passover. As they reclined around the table, Jesus, troubled in spirit, said to them, "One of you shall betray Me." To the everlasting credit of the apostles, they never said, "Oh, I think I know who it is! Peter, I've always had some questions about you." No, they did not suspect each other but simply said, "Lord, is it I?" Matthew reveals that even Judas asked the question along with the rest. But he includes a disclaimer, "Surely not I, Rabbi?" (Matt. 26:25) He decided to play the game with them; they were genuinely asking, "Lord, is it I?" but Judas asked the question

Deceived Into the Wrong Destination

too, and they never suspected his motives. After all, they had seen him witness, perform acts of mercy, and possibly drive out demons. He was as smooth as oil.

Trust Peter to have an overwhelming desire to know the identity of the culprit. So he whispered to John, possibly across the table, "Ask Him who it is." John did so, and Jesus whispered to John so that no one else apparently heard who it was, "It is the one to whom I will give this piece of bread when I have dipped it in the dish" (John 13:26).

The custom was for the host to dip a bit of mutton into sauce and give it to the person on his left, the honored guest. For this Feast of Passover, that person was Judas. Possibly Jesus had even asked Judas to sit next to Him. So as Jesus dipped the mutton into the sauce and gave it to Judas, He was in effect saying, "Judas, do you really want to go through with it? This is your last opportunity to back out of your deal. I am now honoring you and giving you acceptance with the disciples."

Apparently, Judas' mask was so well in place he did not even blush. Nor did he become pale or nervous. He sat calmly, unperturbed. All that he could see flashing in his mind was thirty pieces of silver. No one except Christ knew what was going on in his rebellious, covetous heart. Though Christ was not in his heart, He was on his lips.

As Jesus and the Eleven walked to the Garden of Gethsemane, John may have spread the word to the disciples. Judas, he would have said, was a deceiver.

After prayer, the temple guards appeared, led by Judas. Judas embraced Jesus under the pretense of love, the outward sign, saying, "I adore You." But by that act he was giving a different message to the temple guards: "He is the Man that you have come to arrest and kill. Capture Him."

Judas was so smooth that he made great treachery look like loyalty.

Jesus responded with His characteristic gentleness,

"Friend, do what you came for" (Matt. 26:50). He did not appear to be angry, and of course He wasn't surprised. The deed had been done.

Judas was home free. He had the thirty pieces of silver, a good hedge against inflation and hard times. Sure, Jesus was in custody, but so what? He probably would have been arrested anyway. If you can make a buck, why not?

But suddenly Judas was happy no longer. When he saw that Jesus had been condemned, remorse filled his heart. He returned to the chief priests and elders and handed back the thirty pieces of silver saying, "I have sinned, for I have betrayed innocent blood" (Matt. 27:4).

Their response? "What is that to us? That's your responsibility" (v. 4). Seeing their cold indifference to his emotional anguish, he threw the money into the temple, left, and hanged himself.

The facade was broken. Judas had enough sensitivity to experience remorse, but not enough to experience repentance. Remorse doesn't lead to repentance if you have a hard heart. Judas had never believed in Christ; he went to hell rather than heaven.

Though the covetousness in Judas' heart began as small as a sapling, it had grown into a mighty oak. Sin never stays at the same level. Either it grows in power and control, or else its authority is diminished under the power of Jesus Christ. Yielding to temptation is like throwing a piece of meat to a small but ferocious tiger. He craves satisfaction, promising that just one more morsel is all he wants, but the next day he returns for more, and he's stronger than ever.

Judas did not foresee the guilt that would tear him apart inside. Once again we learn that the consequences of sin are hidden from our eyes. People today may say, "I want something in this world; I want it badly. I'm willing to sacrifice in order to get it." And once they've got it, what they thought would taste like dessert becomes as bitter as wormwood.

Deceived Into the Wrong Destination

Remorse can make any pleasure become a pain. Judas experienced it, and suddenly silver lost its glitter. Too bad that he did not expose his remorse in the presence of Christ—the only place where it can be washed away.

Remorse is guilt borne by us apart from Jesus Christ. It's that sense of shame that hides in your heart when you don't receive Christ's forgiveness. Judas was so overcome by it that he did what 25,000 Americans do every year: he committed suicide. As a fulfillment of prophecy, he was unwilling to lay hold of Jesus Christ's forgiveness.

Why did Jesus choose Judas? Possibly it's because Judas represents the whole human race. Jesus wanted to say for generations to come, "This is the heart of man. This is what man is—he has the ability to appear good on the outside, but inside he is rotten."

The wickedness of Judas should not be a surprise. I've known people who have sold Jesus Christ for less than thirty pieces of silver. Because of some petty treasure they hold in their hand, they will not ask Christ to come into their lives. Pride, an offensive remark, or the love of pleasure—there are a hundred and one such excuses weaker than thirty pieces of silver.

PERSONAL LESSONS

Judas reminds us that no position of honor substitutes for personal conversion. It matters not how high you have come up the ladder of respectability; someday you will find that ladder is leaning against the wrong wall! Despite the honor and respect that you may have received, you can have no substitute for conversion if you want to be in heaven rather than hell.

In fact, perhaps the most important lesson that Judas teaches us is this: The gate of hell is next to the gate of heaven. Though he lived next to the Son of God who was able to save him, Judas held back because of a covetous heart.

Scattered throughout the Scriptures are many epitaphs. Over Judas' grave we would have to write the words of Jesus, "It would have been better for him if he had not been born" (Matt. 26:24). How much better if those parents who lived in Kerioth had never conceived this child!

What a tragedy! To think that Judas, who was with Christ for so long, will have to be in hell forever. Like some Sunday School teachers, even some elders and pastors—like some young people who have been brought up in fine Christian homes—yet lost because they have never been born again through faith in Christ; they betray Christ with every hymn they sing, every prayer they pray, and every good deed they do. Though appearing to be one with Him, their hearts are pointed in a different direction.

Since Christ is the only door to heaven, let's not stand next to Him without walking through.

13

Restoring the Fallen As You Begin

Recently, a friend of mine had to resign as pastor because of an adulterous relationship. Within two days after the affair was discovered, he left the area with his wife and family. Now my problem is how to reach out and restore him back to the fellowship of the saints. I find that I am reluctant to get involved. . . . After all, he would have a sense of shame when I get in touch with him. Since he doesn't live next door to me, I can avoid him without effort. And so, if I follow my inclination, I will do nothing.

But should I?

Suppose Moses had knocked on your door on his flight to Midian. Word of his murder of the Egyptian has already swept through your village. But you are distantly related to him through his mother. To take him in is to invite possible death—but he is a friend who needs help. So what do you do?

You're a member of the congregation at Philippi. A friend reports that Demas is in town but does not come to visit his friends. Should you try to find Demas, or is it his responsibility to get in touch with the local assembly?

Believe it or not, the Bible has much to say about restoration. But before we spell it out, let's consider some reasons why we are so often genuinely perplexed as to what we should do.

First, befriending the fallen does appear to be taking a soft approach to sin. If a man sins, he ought to pay for it: if he is restored too easily, we are giving the impression that sin is not all that serious. So we justify our inaction with the belief that the offender is just getting his due.

Second, we may even be afraid of guilt by association. If we are known to be spending time with one who has failed, we may be considered by others as being guilty too. "Birds of a feather flock together."

But perhaps the most important reason we don't get involved is because confrontation is awkward. If there has been moral failure, there is shame. If a marriage is breaking apart, it is difficult for the couple to admit that they are not making it. Just a week ago I phoned some friends who are on the verge of a divorce. The wife answered the phone but refused to speak to me; I felt uneasy, and she obviously did too. Fortunately, her husband came on the line and rescued his wife from an uncomfortable moment. Yet, both of them were, in their own way, reaching out for someone to talk with. Their friends had deserted them; they felt isolated and alone. If I had not made the first move, they certainly would not have done so.

So how can we be of help in putting broken lives together? This summer I bought our daughters an above-the-ground swimming pool. Incredibly, it came in just one small box. When I took out the pieces, they did not look like a pool at all; in fact I thought they never would! But after I enlisted the help of a friend and carefully read the instructions, the pieces which originally looked so unrelated took on a special shape. We soon had our swimming pool with none of the pieces missing.

All of us have known lives like that—just a bundle of unrelated pieces serving no particular purpose. You wish there was an instruction manual to give you some idea where to begin. You also wish that there would be a model to give you the big picture, so that you would know what the final product would be like.

Of course, there is an instruction book, put together by the Author of life. As our Creator, He knows how to make us whole, but we must give Him all the pieces. Sometimes we need others to help us get ourselves together. There is a role for you and me to play in helping our brothers and sisters. And someday we may need their help too. Not a one of us is beyond the possibility of devastating failure.

If a believer is not restored, the strength of the church is weakened. We are soldiers in the same army, members of the same family, and stones in the same building. That's why a believer who doesn't fellowship with others will never grow in the Christian life. Paul, when speaking to the Christians at Colosse, expressed the hope "that they may be encouraged in heart and united in love, so that they may have the full riches of complete understanding, in order that they may know the mystery of God, namely, Christ" (Col. 2:2). Unless believers are united together in Christ's love, they cannot enter into the fullness of God.

Now to God's instruction manual.

Paul answers several questions about restoration in Galatians: "Brothers, if someone is caught in a sin, you who are spiritual should restore him gently. But watch yourself, or you also may be tempted" (6:1).

First, what does the word *restore* mean? The Greek word is used in the New Testament for the mending of nets and for the setting of a broken bone. Unfortunately, there are many believers whose lives have never been mended; there are many broken bones in the body of Christ that have never been properly set. Many fruitful Christians hobble out of joint, never able to gain their spiritual equilibrium. Restoration means that a fallen believer is back in full fellowship with God and the church. Although he may not always be restored to his former ministry, he is befriended and received fully as a member of the body of

As You Begin

believers. That which he needs most of all, namely, the strength of fellow Christians, is his.

Second, who should take the initiative? Paul's answer is "you who are spiritual." Perhaps there is no clearer test of spirituality versus carnality than when a believer is caught in a sin. The carnal Christian is not seriously interested in restoring a wayward brother. He would rather gossip with a spirit of self-righteousness, hoping that the person pays for his sin even to the last farthing. There will be hidden satisfaction in knowing that someone was caught in a trespass. If the sin was one of sensuality, the carnal believer will especially want the offender to get his just penalty. Probably like the elder brother in the story of the prodigal, the carnal believer secretly wishes he could experience the pleasures of the far country too. So the thought that someone has enjoyed the world and gotten by with it arouses his envy. Since the carnal believer feels he has been cheated of these pleasures, he wants to make sure that others do not enjoy them. So his satisfaction is derived from criticizing the one who has fallen; after all, the carnal Christian feels just a bit taller when he is able to compare himself with his fallen comrade.

The spiritual person will react with sorrow. He will not allow detrimental words to pass his lips. He knows that if a brother has been wounded, then he has been wounded too. He is sensitive and realizes that if a broken bone is not set properly, it may never heal the way it should. More importantly, he knows that his own heart could commit the same sin given the right circumstances. He knows that the only difference between himself and others is the grace of God.

The spiritual believer, then, should take the initiative. It is both unbiblical and cruel to expect that the one who failed should seek out other believers. The one who has sinned feels rejection; he doesn't know whether believers will receive him back or not. His guilt and shame keep driving him farther from those he desperately needs. The spiritual believer should, therefore, take the initiative.

The third question builds on the second: How should one go? "With a spirit of gentleness." If a person has a broken bone, he does not want it pushed into place with a crowbar. That's why the carnal believer is not the one to go, even if he would be glad to. He will only add to the man's guilt; he will increase the alienation his brother already feels. Instead of using salve for the wound, he will use salt.

If a sin has been committed, the offender must be willing to repent. Then, whenever possible, there must be restitution. Often the restoration process must be done in stages, so that there is satisfactory evidence that the offender has admitted the error of his ways.

And if the person does not repent? Jesus put it this way: "If your brother sins against you, go and show him his fault, just between the two of you. If he listens to you, you have won your brother over. But if he will not listen, take one or two others along, so that every matter may be established by the testimony of two or three witnesses. If he refuses to listen to them, tell it to the church; and if he refuses to listen even to the church, treat him as you would a pagan or a tax collector" (Matt. 18:15-17).

So if a person is unwilling to acknowledge his sin, he must be cut off from the fellowship of believers with a clear understanding that he is put under the domain of Satan in order that he might be brought to repentance. Once again, the purpose of such discipline is to bring about reconciliation.

Of course, there are many instances where we ought to restore each other even though no sin has been committed. Here is a man who has failed at his job in the face of high expectations. He thought this was the break he had been waiting for. Everyone knew of his promotion. But all of his dreams ended in disaster. Now he is alone and feels as if he cannot look his friends in the eye. Someone must go and let him know that he is still loved and welcomed as a friend.

This, then, is our role as believers. We are to do all that we can to help one another stay in fellowship with God and

As You Begin

His people. Sometimes it's difficult for those who have been living with wrong attitudes for many years to be restored to fellowship. Satan wants us to think that we have made such a heavy investment in our present course that we cannot change the direction of our lives. But of course we can!

Let us go out of our way to restore someone today. *It's never too late to do what is right!* I am taking that necessary step to contact my pastor friend mentioned in the opening of this chapter. Should you reach out to someone who needs you?